14

new | ECCLESIOLOGY & POLITY

new ECCLESIOLOGY & POLITY

THE UNITED CHURCH OF CHRIST

CLYDE J. STECKEL

THE
PILGRIM
PRESS
Cleveland

The Pilgrim Press
700 Prospect Avenue
Cleveland, Ohio 44115-1100
thepilgrimpress.com

Printed in the United States of America on acid-free paper

13 12 11 10   11 10 9 8

Library of Congress Cataloging-in-Publication Data
Steckel, Clyde J.
  New ecclesiology & polity : the United Church of Christ / Clyde Steckel.
      p. cm.
  Includes bibliographical references.
  ISBN 978-0-8298-1857-4 (alk. paper)
    1. United Church of Christ – Doctrines. 2. United Church of Christ –
Government. 3. Church. 4. Church polity. I. Title. II. Title: New
ecclesiology and polity.
  BX9886.S74 2009
  262′.05834 – dc22
                                                    2009019675

Contents

Introduction
7

CHAPTER ONE
How Polity Impedes Mission
11

CHAPTER TWO
How UCC Ecclesiology and Polity
Became Entangled with Modernity
and Why It Matters
31

CHAPTER THREE
A Re-Visioned Ecclesiology
for Postmodern Times
71

CHAPTER FOUR
A Revised UCC Polity
for Postmodern Times
110

Afterword
140

Notes
143

Introduction

Mainline denominations, like the United Church of Christ, continue to lose members, congregations, financial support, and public influence. Many explanations are offered: the increasing irrelevance of denominational traditions, the secularizing of Western civilization along with the recent rise of militant atheism, the related fear that religion leads to fanaticism and violence, the apparently growing appeal of conservative religion that offers clarity and certainty in an ambiguous world, along with the way homosexuality and other divisive issues preoccupy the mainline churches.

Whatever merit there may be in these assessments and their implied remedies, one explanation is missing: the way the ecclesiology and polity of the United Church of Christ (and other mainline denominations) impede its life and mission in an increasingly postmodern world. Instead of asking how the polity of the denomination could be reshaped to facilitate mission in a postmodern time, we seem bent on further clarifications and refinements in our traditional polity of covenant relations, a polity that is firmly grounded in modernist assumptions and values, less and less relevant in a postmodern world.

I argue in this book that United Church of Christ ecclesiology (the doctrine of the church) and its polity (how the church is organized and operates) urgently need to be reexamined and reshaped if the church is to minister faithfully in a postmodern world. I will describe the transition from modernity to postmodernity, focusing on ways the United Church of Christ, and other mainline denominations, demonstrate a keen awareness of these transitions in many aspects of church life, but virtually no awareness of how denominational governing structures and their theological justifications undermine faithful mission in a postmodern world.

Whether the United Church of Christ can serve as a case study for other mainline denominations, I will let readers judge. In spite of diverse and cherished historic traditions, mainline denominations are more alike than we might want to admit. In governance the UCC is positioned somewhere between presbyterial and congregational systems with its polity of covenant relations, in which national, regional, and local governance structures and their officers are obliged to consult and persuade in relations with one another but cannot constitutionally prescribe or command the outcome of a contended issue. Even in polities where bishops or assemblies have official authority, a consultative style is practiced in order to avoid the fallout from apparently arbitrary decisions. Thus a United Church of Christ case study about modernist polity in a postmodern world might be more widely useful. I hope it is.

In this book I will, in the first chapter, describe how the ecclesiology and polity of the United Church of Christ seriously impede its life and mission in the world. As someone who has written about and taught UCC ecclesiology and polity for many years, this will be an especially painful exercise, since I love my church and have believed that its ecclesiology and polity have been close to the core of its identity. If that is so, it is now time to acknowledge the deficits of that identity and work for its transformation.

In the second chapter I will explain how the ecclesiology and polity of the United Church of Christ were shaped out of Protestant Reformation and Enlightenment beliefs that held sway in Western civilization until the mid-twentieth century, a consensus to which we cling in spite of the erosion and eventual disintegration of modernity in the late twentieth century. This will require definitions of modernity and postmodernity that will have to be compact but, I hope, clear and persuasive nevertheless.

The third chapter contains revisions needed in ecclesiology so that the United Church of Christ can more faithfully minister in postmodernity. These revisions will include a new interpretation of the claim that Jesus Christ is the sole head of the church, and how that headship is exercised in the church. Universality and apostolic fidelity, ancient marks of the true church, will need to be added to United Church of Christ ecclesiology, in keeping with its commitment to the unity of the church. The Reformation norms of word and sacrament will need further elaboration in a revised ecclesiology. Speaking of the church as engaged in "the mission of God," a widely used phrase these days to express the essence of the church, will need to be revised to include the communal and inner life of the church and not just its actions for peace and justice in the world. The church as covenant community, also a widely used ecclesiological theme, will require both theological and practical clarification about the consequences of breaking the covenant. And the newly emerging identity theme of the "still-speaking God" will require an ecclesiological context in which new words from God will be tested by their congruence with biblical and specifically christological norms.

The fourth and final chapter presents needed revisions in the polity of the United Church of Christ in keeping with the demands of postmodernity and the revisions in ecclesiology of the previous chapter. These include the creation of conference-based church and ministry boards, where appointments will be for longer terms of service than typically those of present committees on the ministry, and where board membership will require professional preparation and be modestly remunerated. Some constitutional and bylaw revisions will be required to take this step. The authority and role of the conference minister also requires substantial revision, with not only pastoral and persuasive authority but also a strengthened oversight authority to intervene with authorized ministers, local churches, and other ministry settings where the well-being of the church and its ministry is compromised. This enhancement of the authority of conference ministers will require constitutional and bylaw revisions, as well as discussion and discernment across the life of the church.

CHAPTER ONE

How Polity Impedes Mission

THE FOUNDERS OF THE UNITED CHURCH OF CHRIST created a governance structure, another word for which is polity, which included both the principle of the autonomy of the local church dear to Congregationalists, and the presbyterial church order of the Evangelical and Reformed Church, where synods and the General Synod made authoritative decisions on behalf of the whole church. It was this constitutional authority to speak and act on behalf of the whole church that worried Congregationalists over a loss of autonomy that might lie ahead in a union with the Evangelical and Reformed Church. To reassure wary Congregationalists the Commission to Prepare a Constitution wrote the constitutional paragraph (originally Paragraph 15, now Paragraph 18) that guaranteed the right of the local church to determine its own beliefs, create its own confessions or covenants, worship as it saw fit, and own and dispose of its own real property without the permission or interference of the wider church. In an effort to maintain traditional Congregational practices and something of the spirit of Evangelical and Reformed presbyterial polity, however, these sweeping affirmations of local church autonomy were balanced in the Constitution by Paragraphs 17 and 19 calling for the mutual respect of actions by local churches, associations, conferences, and the General Synod and its related bodies — that all such actions should be received with respect, taken seriously, and given thoughtful and prayerful response.

This effort to balance traditional polities did not, however, in the years immediately after the union in 1957, result either in a clear definition of a new polity as hoped for by the founders, or in a balanced and nuanced interim polity that honored both Congregational and Evangelical and Reformed traditions. The Evangelical and Reformed heritage of a constitutional synodical authority soon disappeared. Congregationalist autonomy won the day, even though many Congregationalists continued to worry about a hierarchical church order lurking in the wings.

In the midst of this mix of confusion, dashed hopes, and the triumph of one polity tradition over the other, an old word emerged, covenant, put to a new use to characterize and explain the polity of the UCC and to distinguish it from congregational, presbyterial, or episcopal polities. In the speeches and writings of Robert Moss and Avery Post, UCC presidents in the 1970s, and Louis Gunnemann, seminary dean and historian, as well as Ruben Sheares, executive director of the Office for Church Life and Leadership, that word, covenant, was increasingly employed to define UCC polity. The idea of "covenant" was rich with biblical and theological resonance especially cherished in the New England Congregationalist and German Reformed traditions. Since biblical covenants were initiated by a gracious God, the church could view its polity not simply as a humanly devised system of governance, but as promises made between God and the followers of Jesus Christ to live and govern themselves as God would have it done. This belief in a divine origination of polity corresponded closely to historic Reformed and Free Church traditions, where church governance and, in the Reformed case, the governance of the city or state were understood to be guided by God's Spirit according to a divine plan. Gradually the language of covenant caught on, appearing increasingly in revised editions of the *Manual on Ministry,* and eventually in the constitutional revisions of 2000, where a new Article III, headed Covenantal Relationships, declares that all expressions of the church have " . . . responsibilities and rights in relation to the others, to that end that the whole church will seek God's will and be faithful to God's mission. Decisions are made in consultation and collaboration among the various parts of the structure."

Three emerging themes in UCC identity in the late twentieth century and the early twenty-first century have important implications for ecclesiology and polity, though these implications have not been worked out as fully as the ecclesiology affirming that the church is headed solely by Jesus Christ and the polity of covenant relations. These three themes are those about diversity (the commitment to be a church that is multicultural, multiracial, just peace, open and affirming, and accessible to all), about the church engaged in the mission of God, and about the church as a community hearing and bearing witness to the still-speaking God.

Affirming diversity would seem agreeable to historic UCC affirmations about the church and its polity of covenant relations, if diversities of culture, race, gender, sexual orientation, and abilities are viewed as gifts of the Creator. Many in the Christian world, including the UCC, would not agree with that claim, however, particularly on gender and sexual orientation. Within the UCC conflicts over homosexuality persist in spite of studies and actions by the General Synod and other expressions of the church that affirm the rights of lesbian, gay, bisexual, and transgender persons to full equality before the law and to church membership and ordination. Within the wider Christian family, even deeper divisions over sexual orientation threaten the unity of historic denominations. And in many traditions, gender equality and the possibility of ordination are decisively rejected. Diversity of cultures poses an additional challenge to UCC core convictions, especially where cultural traditions reject gender equality or homosexuality. How far can the UCC go in welcoming cultural traditions that reject such core UCC affirmations? It is difficult even to have a conversation on such a question, let alone come to any agreement.

A second ecclesiological and polity theme — the church called to engage in the "mission of God" — is now widely employed in the United Church of Christ. While the phrase comes from the writings of David Bosch, the notion of the church as mission goes back to the beginnings of the Christian movement, first as a politically subversive religious movement in the Roman

Empire, then as the official religion of that empire. In those officially Christian centuries of medieval and modern times, empire and religion worked hand in hand to Christianize the peoples under their joint rule. In the modern era of world exploration and colonization by Western nations, missionary movements imposed European and American cultural values and Christian faith, often uncritically mixed together, to bring Latin American, Asian, and African peoples into political and religious subordination. But this unholy alliance began to break down in the early twentieth century as the worldwide ecumenical movement fostered the increasing autonomy and equality of missionary and established churches and as critical theological analysis in Western churches challenged the centuries-long alliance of church and society. In this critique the meaning of mission was radically transformed. The mission of the church, the mission of Jesus Christ, was to bear witness against the injustices of society and to call for social transformation in keeping with God's righteousness and peace, even if the consequences were a marginalization of the church as institution or, beyond that, martyrdom. Using Bosch's ecumenically more inclusive phrase, the mission of God, the United Church of Christ now understands itself as a church called to God's mission on behalf of the world, not primarily on behalf of the church or the individual believer. The "mission of God" phrase now appears widely in UCC discourse — for example, in the documents concerning the restructuring of 2000, and now in the Pronouncement on Ministry adopted by General Synod 25. This worldly emphasis, with the church understood as faithful followers of Christ engaged in God's mission on behalf of the world, places the institutional life of the church and the pilgrimage of the individual believer in an instrumental role for the sake of God's mission, not as ends in and of themselves.

The affirmation that God is still speaking, that one should never place a period where God has placed a comma, is a third and more recent UCC theme bearing implications for ecclesiology and polity. This identity campaign, with its TV commercials, visually integrated media materials, including identity items like pins, shirts, mugs, bumper stickers, and the like, makes it clear that all are welcome in the UCC, that even if the preponderance of Christian interpretation of scripture lines up against homosexuality, God is speaking a new word in this time, a word of welcome and affirmation for persons of LGBT orientation, and that the faithful church should be attentive to that word, and not simply to interpretations of the ancient words. What this affirmation does not address, however, is the question of discerning claims on behalf of other new words by the still-speaking God. How will the church tell if new words claiming to be from God are truly of divine origin? Pentecostalism has not been a core characteristic of the UCC, but some notion of continuing revelation is consistent with its liberal theological heritage. As long as God's new words are primarily those of welcome where the church previously excluded people, such questions may be beside the point. But surely if God keeps on speaking, this divine speech may not always be words of welcome and affirmation. God's words may be about judgment. What then? Will modernist ecclesiology and polity be adequate for such discernment?

This emerging ecclesiology and its polity in process are clearly grounded in Free Church Reformation theological principles and in modern Enlightenment political and philosophical beliefs. These two sources are remarkably in harmony, as I will show later, but this is a harmony that today impedes the mission of the church in the postmodern world, however well suited it might have been to modernity. First, though, the strengths of this current UCC ecclesiology and polity ought to be recognized and clearly stated. There will be losses as well as gains if the UCC revises its ecclesiology and polity in ways I am proposing, so current strengths inherent in UCC ecclesiology and polity need to be identified and weighed in the balance.

One of the obvious strengths of UCC ecclesiology and polity is their permission, even encouragement of initiative by anyone, literally — individuals, local churches, associations, conferences, the General Synod and other national bodies — to speak and act on matters of concern in church and society. As long as these statements and actions are within the domain of the responsibility of that person or body, as understood in common practice or as defined in the Constitution, no other permission must be sought. This does not mean an absence of consultation or a failure to attempt persuading others to join in the statement or action. But it does mean that action does not need to await consensus or majority vote by the whole church. While it is clear to those familiar with the Constitution and the practice of the church that no one can speak *for* the UCC, it is also clear that often these prophetic and courageous actions are identified as coming from United Church of Christ expressions, especially when it is the General Synod or the General Minister and President, and therefore, in the public view, are assumed to represent the UCC. Though it is constitutionally accurate it is also a bit disingenuous to say that no such body or person can speak for the UCC. An officer or official body would have to disavow their UCC identity to claim that they speak only *to* the church and not, in some fashion, on its behalf. This confusion is exacerbated by the fact that the General Synod is composed, in part, of delegates elected by the conferences, so that it looks and acts like a representative governing body, even though it is not that in any strict constitutional sense. A further tension arising from this polity of initiative and persuasion, now widely understood as a polity of covenant, is the situation where UCC stances are not widely supported, when significant numbers of members, clergy, or local churches disagree with UCC "official viewpoints" (such language is not appropriate but is still widely used), and then believe that their contrary views were not expressed, or not heard, or not treated with respect. Some dissidents leave the UCC. Others organize movements to challenge and change these stances. Such disaffections should not be taken lightly. But surely this kind of polity has a flexibility and strength not seen these days in other mainline denominations, where deep divisions and the risk of schism over issues relating to sexual orientation — ordination, equality of marriage as defined in law, etc. — cannot be readily resolved where some official or representative governing body finally has to say yes or no on these issues, a decision that is binding for the whole denomination.

A second obvious strength of a polity of covenant, as increasingly understood and practiced in the UCC, is its reliance on persuasion, patience, and prayerful discernment instead of majority vote or executive fiat. Decisions are sometimes painfully slow in such a polity, and some decisions still need to be made quickly. It is also difficult for decisive and impatient persons to work comfortably in such a polity. Sometimes their gifts are lost simply because they decide not to stay with it. But surely the benefits of patient persuasion and prayerfulness outweigh, in most instances, those of quick and firm decisions. What is less clear, so far, is how a polity of covenant treats those who do not get it, who do not seem to understand the rules, or who choose not to play by the rules. What are the consequences of breaking the covenant? In the biblical and theological framework in which a polity of covenant has been set, breaking the covenant is punished by dire consequences like war, famine, flood, fire, illness, or death. Today, however, one dare not view such outcomes as God's punishments. To do so would make God a harsh and vindictive despot, not the loving and compassionate God known in Jesus Christ.

In the absence of such rewards-or-punishments theology, a polity of covenant can rely only on pleas and admonitions. If an individual, a local church, or some other ecclesiastical entity chooses to ignore pleas or admonitions from covenant partners, no consequences can be legitimately applied by covenant partners, except in the cases of the standing of local churches or authorized ministers. Association committees on the ministry have become more careful about ministerial standing in view of an increased public awareness of clergy misconduct or abuse, but have still not systematically or intentionally reviewed the standing of local churches even though they are authorized to do so in the Constitution of the United Church of Christ. From this reluctance to impose penalties, even when constitutionally authorized to do so, the covenantal polity of the UCC becomes an exercise of moral exhortation rather than a system of rewards and penalties for keeping or breaking the covenant. It seems that is about all that can be done.

And the United Church of Christ's welcome of diversity in cultural, racial, or ethnic heritage, or in sexual orientation, shows the strength of an ecclesiology and polity open to new messages from the still-speaking God. While there are biblical testimonies to God's inclusive love that is impartial, there is no similarly clear biblical embrace of diverse sexual orientation or marriage between persons of the same gender. If one has to depend on clear biblical warrants or biblical silence to permit such affirmations, there is a problem. But if God is still speaking, then a new truth hitherto unimagined can be discerned and embraced, so long as its spirit is in keeping with core faith affirmations. If the United Church of Christ and other Christian communions cannot entertain that possibility, then no radically new message from God can be allowed. UCC ecclesiology and polity make that discernment of new divine truth possible. It is more difficult in other ecclesiologies and polities.

With these strengths of UCC ecclesiology and polity I have just discussed, it may seem an act of perverse folly to argue that this ecclesiology and polity of the United Church of Christ impede its mission, but that is precisely what I have come to believe. These impediments are grounded in the transition from modernity to postmodernity now under way in Western culture. I will next outline these impediments and then, in the next chapter, explain more fully the transition from modernity to postmodernity.

In United Church of Christ ecclesiology, there is a structural contradiction built into the Constitution that makes it impossible to state what the UCC believes. Paragraph 2 of the Preamble summarizes UCC beliefs about Jesus Christ as sole head of the church as well as Son of God and Savior, about the Word of God in the scriptures, the historic faith of the church set forth in the ancient creeds and Protestant Reformation insights, the admonition that each generation needs to make this faith its own in "reality of worship, in honesty of thought and expression, and in purity of heart before God," and the recognition of two sacraments: Baptism and the Lord's Supper.

But in Paragraph 18, within Article V, which speaks of Local Churches, the autonomy of the local church is declared to be "inherent and modifiable only by its own action." Among the rights of the local church guaranteed against encroachment by the General Synod, association, conference, or any other body are the right to "retain or adopt its own methods of organization, worship and education; to retain or secure its own charter and name; to adopt its own constitution and bylaws; to formulate its own covenants and confessions of faith." While these absolute rights of autonomous local churches are set within a context of Paragraph 6 calling for the practice of covenantal relations and Paragraphs 17 and 19 asserting the responsibility of local churches to care for the whole church and to hold in the highest regard decisions or advice from the General Synod as well as their conferences and associations, these are relatively weak admonitions when placed alongside the absolute protections contained in Paragraph 18.

In practice this contradiction has required precise definitions (not always grasped within the UCC or by the public, the media, or dialogue partners) of which body is speaking, and for whom it is speaking (only themselves) when any expression of the United Church of Christ makes a public pronouncement on issues of the day, or engages in ecumenical or interfaith dialogue. Paragraph 18 means that, literally, only the whole church (every local church, every other expression of the church) can speak with authority about any matter of faith or practice. There is, to put it another way, no authoritative teaching office in the United Church of Christ except for the whole church. Other denominations specify bishops, or councils, or synods as authoritative teaching offices. The UCC identifies only itself, its whole self, as qualified to determine what it believes and how it is to act.

The current transition from modernity to postmodernity in Western culture stretches and even breaks this persisting tension between autonomy and covenant relations of mutual consultation. When the dominant values and assumptions in Western culture held sway — values like the autonomous self, reasoned consideration and persuasion, government by the consent of the governed, authority and power shared with equity, and the inherent respect due all persons — a UCC ecclesiology and polity embracing these values could be made to work even though key constitutional paragraphs seemed contradictory. One could not imagine that an autonomous local church would exercise its right to determine its own confessions or covenants of faith (Paragraph 18) in a manner that would directly contradict Paragraph 2 in the Preamble. A sampling of local church mission or vision statements, however, or ordination papers coming to committees on the ministry would show only a distant echo of affirmations taken for granted in the Preamble. This puzzling and disturbing state of affairs arises, I would argue, more from the difficult transitions from modernity to postmodernity than from any lack of rigorous seminary teaching or any loss of due diligence by committees on the ministry.

Two other examples illustrate the difficulties inherent in this transition: one is the decision of a local church to leave the denomination (not a uniquely UCC risk) after a number of newer members join and, sooner or later, occupy key offices and have enough votes to prevail over those who wish to stay in the denomination. And the second example consists of the road-blocks in the way of becoming a multicultural and multiracial church, especially in most local congregations, as the General Synod has declared the United Church of Christ committed to becoming. Each example needs to be interpreted from many viewpoints, but here I will focus on the transition from modernity to postmodernity to show how the UCC is ill-equipped in its ecclesiology and polity to meet these challenges.

In the example of the local church taken over by new members who, for whatever reasons, organize themselves into a sufficiently powerful political force to remove the church from the denomination, the assumptions of modernity would imagine that new members would be gradually incorporated into the culture and traditions of the local church, would come to own its covenant and become as loyal as the previous members, and, particularly if coming from another denomination, would learn the traditions and current stances of the UCC and would honor them, even if they appear new or controversial. This all would take place, modernity would assume, under the leadership of denominationally informed and committed clergy and lay leaders. Ongoing education, abundant information, and a steady stream of conversation about what is believed and why it is believed would eventually initiate these new members or, if the differences were too great, encourage them to look for another church.

In postmodernity, however, such governing assumptions and values have drastically changed. Belief is a matter of individual choice. One is not to judge the beliefs of others. New members filled with enthusiasm and willing to invest many hours of volunteer time are welcomed by tired and burnt-out older members. For a while a new atmosphere of enthusiasm replaces the low energy level that prevailed in recent years. The identity of the local church is only faintly formed in its historic denominational traditions, while a new identity of evangelical fervor comes to the fore. If the pastor retires, the search for a new pastor will be shaped by the expectations of these newer members, resulting, possibly, in using an Internet search or a private consulting firm rather than denominational channels. A new minister is called who fits the bill, even though his or her denominational background may be uncertain or unclear to the members. The new minister's preaching is filled with just the kind of passion the former minister lacked or had lost. New people are attending and then joining the church. More money is appearing in the offering plates. What better time is it to consider severing a denominational connection that asks for money for distant mission projects but does not seem to provide many other services?

How is postmodernity seen in this example? In two ways: the license to organize and take over an existing church with an apparently clear conscience, even a self-righteous conscience, is an example of the ideological passion and purity that flourish in postmodernity, where the assumptions and values of modernity no longer prevail and no longer provide widely shared values and rules of conduct. Second, postmodernity is displayed in the uncertainty of the longer-term members of this vulnerable local church, and perhaps even in the denominational bodies and officials to which the church has been connected, about what to say or what to do in the face of such a blatant arrogation of unchecked power. The confidence about the theological identity of such a local church has, perhaps, receded behind a genial tolerance that wants to avoid open conflict at all costs, and is therefore unable to stand up against the bullying tactics of a new majority. Ideological passion and purity running roughshod over an identity of getting along by avoiding conflict — these are sure signs of the unraveling of the dominant social contract as well as ecclesiastical covenants in postmodernity.

A second example of the way the United Church of Christ modernist ecclesiology and polity impede the mission of the UCC is seen in the difficulty many congregations have when they try to become multiracial and multicultural, in keeping with General Synod declarations. This is particularly ironic because commitments to diversity and to being multiracial and multicultural are distinctly postmodern declarations, standing against the homogenizing and leveling tendencies of modernity, against the melting pot and affirming a diverse stew of interesting and valuable variations. But many local churches seem blocked by geography and population groups in their communities from attaining any significant degree of racial or cultural diversity. Even local churches with diversity all around them do not readily embrace diversity, as Laurene Beth Bowers has demonstrated in *Becoming a Multicultural Church*.[1] Old habits persist but must be examined and deconstructed if change is to occur. Charismatic leadership is crucial to success, Bowers declares. In an ecclesiology and polity where authority to a significant degree arises from the people, it will be difficult for people who are unconsciously and unintentionally racist, sexist, homophobic, and classist to repent and change their ways in a manner that does not protect their old and comforting insularity. Even where a local church is able to attract a token multiracial or multicultural membership, pressures will be strong to blend them into the old modernist ways rather than opening the local church to newer postmodern vistas.

In marked contrast with these local church difficulties in becoming truly diverse, a fully multiracial and multicultural church can be seen in the national setting of the United Church of

Christ, where the General Synod, the Executive Council, and the covenanted ministries elect and appoint sufficient numbers of racially and culturally diverse board members and staff to be truly multiracial and multicultural. It is this diversity that makes national meetings and bodies exciting and empowering to those who become involved, and that also makes many local churches seem dull and monochromatic in contrast. Some conferences and associations are able to be more inclusive and diverse than their local churches, but many are not.

What then can the local church do? Working for a diverse local church membership as a goal puts an undue burden of responsibility for a diverse church identity on whatever number of multiracial members a church can attract, since it is hoped that they will enter into the existing local church culture. They may be exuberantly welcomed, even privileged in their participation, while at the same time restive under the expectation that they are to represent their racial or cultural group — a narrowly defined role if one is seeking a full-orbed experience of church membership. At the same time, the dominant and previously existing local church culture will resist the fundamental changes required of a truly diverse church and may even feel smug about becoming multiracial and multicultural without having to change very much. Anti-racism and white privilege educational programs address such self-righteousness directly and effectively. But in the UCC version of a modern ecclesiology and polity, such programs must be sold and entered into voluntarily, which means that only those with already sensitized consciences are likely prospects. Those "who need such programs the most," as we frequently say, those covert racists and monoculturalists who view themselves as liberal in spirit but resist looking inside the fortress of white privilege, will probably not enroll in such programs, or if they do, they will turn the class into a debating society.

A postmodern ecclesiology and polity might establish such anti-racism and white privilege experiences as requirements for the continued good standing of a local church or even as a prescribed discipline for church members to remain in good standing. Like ordered Sunday worship with preaching and prayer and sacramental observances, or like boundary training already required in some associations and conferences, anti-racism training could be another required course in the total curriculum of church life, not an elective. While it is hard to imagine such an outcome within the present UCC ecclesiology and polity of modernity, it should surely be possible to discuss, at least, such prospects as we become more aware of the transition from modernity to a postmodern ecclesiology and polity.

Oversight of authorized ministers (UCC language for ordained, commissioned, and licensed ministers) and of local churches is another mission arena where our modern UCC ecclesiology and polity get in the way. This oversight is officially entrusted to associations (or conferences acting as associations), although in practice committees on the ministry exercise that authority on behalf of associations. Conference and association ministers also play crucial advisory roles in oversight, though without specific constitutional authorization. Article VI of the Constitution and Article I of the Bylaws set forth these ministry oversight responsibilities of associations without speaking of committees on the ministry. Foundational ecclesiological affirmations and polity practices have been set forth in the *Manual on Ministry*. Though having no constitutional authority, the *Manual* has been officially adopted by many associations and conferences acting as associations as the policies and procedures their committees on the ministry will follow. The oversight practiced by these committees on the ministry, following the guidance of the *Manual,* include the counseling of persons in care, as they move toward ordination, commissioning, or licensing; calling ecclesiastical councils to consider candidates for ordination; facilitating preparation for ordinations and installations; consulting with search committees in local churches and other ministry settings as they seek new leaders; the continuing supervision of authorized ministers; and, when necessary, disciplinary actions where complaints are lodged.

While Paragraph 18 of the Constitution makes it clear that congregations can legally call whomever they will to be their pastors, Paragraph 6 on covenantal relations makes it quite clear that to honor covenant relations, authorized ministers and local churches or other ministry settings need to receive and embrace the oversight provided by committees on the ministry. But still the practice of oversight, while strongly urged, is finally a voluntary arrangement. Local churches do, indeed, go their own way by calling pastors who might not be approved by a committee on the ministry. When that happens, there is little the association or committee on the ministry can do. Sometimes these irregularly called pastors actively lead or passively permit an initiative in the congregation to withdraw from the denomination altogether. Again there is not much that the association can do.

In the midst of this anomalous situation of a voluntary system of oversight, the authority of conference ministers and association ministers is also compromised. These are usually the first persons called when a church is divided or unhappy with its pastor, or with the denomination, but beyond a pastoral role of listening, suggesting, and advising, these conference and association ministers have no official basis to act. They must consult and then work with committees on the ministry to address concerns brought by churches or clergy. Conference or association ministers who stay long enough in one place sometimes earn sufficient respect and affection to exercise pastoral authority to which they are not officially entitled. But with the relatively short tenures of most such conference and association ministers, those possibilities are infrequently realized.

The sharply limited and poorly defined authority of the Collegium of Officers of the United Church of Christ — General Minister and President, Associate General Minister, and the Executive Ministers of Justice and Witness Ministries, Local Church Ministries, and Wider Church Ministries — illustrate how the mission of the church is compromised by its modernist assumptions and values. Calling this body a Collegium of Officers, as stated in the constitutional changes of 2000, creates confusion in the wider church and among the officers themselves about the kind of authority the church grants to the General Minister and President. Each officer represents a board, a staff, and program activities on behalf of the whole church. What does that leave the General Minister and President? Is that office only administrative? Is it a ceremonial office like presidents in European parliamentary democracies? Or is it an office with real authority in relation to the other executive ministers? And who would decide? Calling these officers collectively a collegium suggests that all decisions will be made collegially, and that the General Minister and President is simply one among many. But the words "General Minister and President," suggest otherwise, that this office has a breadth of authority and responsibility not inherently found in the other executive ministers. These semantic confusions and their underlying power struggles nicely illustrate the baleful effects of modernist assumptions and values, where everyone is presumed to have a good-hearted balance of concern for their own domains and the whole church, where it is believed that reasoned discussion will produce decisions genuinely embraced by all participants, and where any centralized leadership is both consciously rejected and unconsciously resisted.

These weaknesses in ecclesiastical oversight typical of the United Church of Christ could be traced to poor design or to poorly chosen leaders. Within a modernist paradigm the remedies would be redesigning the present system or changing the way leaders are selected. And this is indeed what we attempt when things are not working well. We engage in expensive and time-consuming restructuring processes. And we redesign and reconfigure executive staff positions. But little seems to change. I am arguing, contrary to those familiar responses, that we must examine the deeper changes from modernist to postmodern culture going on around us, including in our churches. Only then can we get beyond tinkering with systems that are malfunctioning or already broken down.

The modernist flaws in this present system of oversight include the belief that people are reasonable and will be persuaded to change by reasoned argument; that a voluntary system of oversight works best because consent must be won but can never be coerced; and that however much time it takes, a voluntary resolution of disputes will always be better than one made in haste without sufficient study or discussion. But what if these cherished beliefs in UCC ecclesiology and polity were simply not true, or what if their truth claims were limited by contextual constraints? A modernist would insist that people are inherently rational beings, that reason is the characteristic elevating humankind above other living beings, that enlightened reason will enable people to choose and act for what is best for the individual and society (with the implied belief that all people are alike in these regards, whatever their cultural heritage), and that the discovery of new knowledge brings progress to the human enterprise because new decisions will be better informed than earlier ones.

A postmodernist would argue, against those modernist claims, that reason is neither universal nor value-free, but that it functions to create coherent patterns of meaning justifying the special interests and needs of groups. These coherent patterns of meaning may be shaped by religious or philosophical or political convictions about what is best for them and society. That these convictions are grounded in history and the emotions as much as in a supposedly value-free reasoned analysis, and any universalizing worldview, like a Western Enlightenment perspective, is inherently coercive and inhumane for all those not holding power. And while a postmodernist would recognize that progress occurs in many human endeavors, there is also regression, so that progress cannot be the dominant narrative in human history.

I offer as the last illustration of the ways a modernist ecclesiology and polity impede the church's mission a consideration of how we engage in the discernment and formation of church leaders, especially professional leaders, or as we say in the UCC, "authorized ministers." The dominant UCC tradition of an educated clergy, bequeathed by our Protestant Reformation ancestors, has become crystallized into the requirement of a collegiate bachelor's degree and a graduate divinity degree, the M.Div.

When the United Church of Christ came into being in 1957, however, two dimensions of its heritage were at odds with this

Enlightenment consensus: the presence of the historical Christian Connection and Afro-Christian congregations through the union of Congregationalists and Christians in 1921, and the increasing influence of Neo-orthodox theology in mainstream denominations, a theology that criticized the conformity of the church to modern liberal culture in its democratic and capitalist expressions. While Neo-orthodoxy was eventually domesticated in varied political and liberation theologies, the presence of the Christian Connection and Afro-Christian traditions raised difficult questions for those believing in a learned clergy, which meant a college and seminary educated clergy. What was the church to do with clergy who had never been to seminary or even to college? What was the church to do with leaders claiming a calling and formed by the Spirit, in the church, through prayer and Bible study, not through formal graduate study?

These questions were only the beginning. As the UCC attempted to become a multicultural and multiracial church, it welcomed communities and cultures that had never shared the Enlightenment modernist consensus about a learned clergy. Native American, Hispanic American, and Asian American communities valued church leaders spiritually formed in the life of the local community and its culture, not in distant centers of Euro-American-based graduate education. Many African American church communities, even though historically formed in familiar American denominational traditions, also stressed the calling out of their pastors and other church leaders from the home community and its culture.

At the same time small membership congregations in rural and ranching regions of the United States, where economic and population losses are widespread, found it impossible to maintain sufficient membership or income to support full-time ordained pastors with traditional college and seminary degrees. Part-time pastors, often from the local community, with mixed educational backgrounds, increasingly served these churches. Some conferences or regional theological education institutions developed curricula for licensed ministry, with short-term or weekend courses to provide a minimal foundational education.

Until General Synod 25 in 2005, both the UCC discernment, preparation, and placement systems, as well as the *Manual on Ministry,* continued to set forth the expectation that the normative path to a learned ministry included college and seminary degrees. There is also in the *Manual* a comprehensive and fairly traditional list of subjects that should be covered in an education for ordained ministry. The Pronouncement on Ministry adopted by General Synod 25, however, approved three paths to ordained ministry, one with the traditional academic degrees, a second using conference-based or regional educational programs over a seven-year time span, and a third based in a seven-year intentional mentorship program. Though this pronouncement was several years in the making, with diverse study and writing groups engaged in its creation, discussions of what to do about the growing leadership crisis had been taking place for many years.

While this Pronouncement on Ministry with its multiple paths to ordination promised to help move the church beyond a single university-based Enlightenment educational standard, in fact both the Pronouncement and the Guidelines for Implementation (a document still under development) are situated squarely in modernity, not in postmodernity. That is because the knowledge and skills expected of ordained ministers are essentially those of the old *Manual* and the former single path. What is new in the two paths to ordination not grounded in college and seminary degrees is the requirement for new educational delivery systems, either those based regionally in conferences or specialized educational programs, or programs of mentoring, yet to be formally developed. Surely innovative educational delivery systems are needed. But instead of a thorough revision of the knowledge, skills, and personal formation that a truly multicultural and multiracial church in a postmodern world would need, the pronouncement simply passes traditional modernist educational tasks along to committees on the ministry, no longer counting on seminary and college degree programs to carry the major educational burden. In addition to those new assignments for committees on the ministry, the pronouncement expects these committees to monitor existing educational programs and to create completely new ones, particularly for the mentoring track. These committees on the ministry are comprised of lay and clergy members and lose one-third of their membership each year, with a third of new members being added, none of whom may be experienced in evaluating or creating educational programs.

Laying very heavy but still traditional educational obligations on volunteer committees, without any guidance on the paradigm shift from modernity to postmodernity, will, I fear, have the effect of trying to do what we've always done but not doing it as well. Meanwhile the opportunity to envision a radically new leadership formation for new kinds of churches in a new cultural time will slip away, and a modernist Enlightenment paradigm will continue to marginalize the United Church of Christ in a postmodern world.

In this chapter I have outlined the history of United Church of Christ ecclesiology and polity as quintessentially representing the modern spirit. Then I identified the strengths of this ecclesiology and polity when compared to others in the major Western Christian denominational traditions. Finally I examined several arenas where this modernist ecclesiology and polity seriously impede the mission of the United Church of Christ. Along the way I have argued that a study of the emerging postmodern world, as the social and cultural context for all church organizations, suggests ways in which UCC ecclesiology and polity need to be revised.

Before proposing revisions, however, I need to explain more fully the transition from modernity to postmodernity in which we are all caught up, whether we are aware of it or not. That is the task of the next chapter.

CHAPTER TWO

How UCC Ecclesiology and Polity Became Entangled with Modernity and Why It Matters

I F THE UNITED CHURCH OF CHRIST is to revise its ecclesiology and polity for the sake of faithful mission, the church will need to understand how it became entangled with modernity and what the current transition from modernity to postmodernity requires. I address two questions in this chapter: How does the emerging culture of postmodernity make the United Church of Christ and other mainlines less effective in their mission? And how did UCC ecclesiology and polity become entangled with modernity?

First I will describe how Western culture is moving out of modernity into postmodernity and why we need to understand this transition. While observers of cultural change have always analyzed what is changing and why it is changing, the current transition from modernity to postmodernity is such a dramatic and global upheaval that models of gradual evolution no longer work. Political and ideological explanations, with their implied laments and accusations, make it impossible to examine this transition objectively. Conservatives lament the cultural and moral disintegration they blame on the upheavals of the 1960s. Liberals interpret these same changes as an incomplete revolution, with much still to do. Other interpreters emphasize advances in technology or the emergence of a visual media culture edging out a culture of words and ideas. An emerging global economy controlled by Western economies is another expression of a major transition. These examples illustrate how the transition from modernity to postmodernity continues to be organized along familiar political and ideological lines, with postmodernity labeled as liberal or radical while modernity is identified as conservative. In academic circles, especially in literary studies and the humanities, postmodernity means a critique of received texts, like the list of the "great books" of the Western cultural heritage, along with a call to expand this canon by adding texts from marginalized and oppressed cultures of diverse racial, gender, class, or sexual orientations. In liberal divinity schools and theological seminaries, including those of the UCC, this same dynamic prevails: historically traditional texts are rigorously deconstructed, exposing their dominating origins and oppressive consequences for subjugated peoples, while at the same time new texts from oppressed cultures are introduced, texts adding diverse moral and spiritual perspectives. The United Church of Christ, in its General Synod pronouncements on becoming a just peace, multiracial, multicultural, open and affirming church accessible to all, has also aligned itself with postmodernity and has thus been accused in conservative circles of being no more than a "politically correct" church, even though the UCC tries to trace its postmodern convictions to biblical and theological sources.

More difficult than avoiding a politicizing of the transition from modernity to postmodernity is discerning the paradigm shift embedded in this transition. While the word "paradigm" is now widely used to explain large-scale change (a word entering our cultural discourse by way of Thomas Kuhn's book *The Structure of the Scientific Revolution*[2]) we often do not take fully into account the harrowing consequences of dislodging oneself from a familiar worldview in order to adopt a different one. Using the image of a large lens through which all experience is filtered (a lens we share with others in the same culture and society), the idea of a paradigm shift requires, first, acknowledging that there is a lens, that our perceptions are not just "the way things are," and in doing that, stepping back far enough to see the lens itself, as well as everything coming through the lens, and then recognizing that there are other lenses through which the same experiences can be viewed, which make these same experiences look quite different from the way they did before.

The image of a lens does not, however, account for the way a paradigm is embedded in the way experience is viewed and interpreted, as well as embedded in the depths of human awareness, including unconscious dimensions, feelings, attitudes, and values. The very constitution of our collective and individual selfhood is woven into the dominant cultural paradigm in which we live, and we learn from early childhood to assume that this is indeed the way things are, that they could not be otherwise. It is only from troubling experiences of some strange "otherness" that we catch a glimmer of alternative worlds, a glimmer we try to suppress and forget. If, for example, we have learned to fear and hate persons from a different racial or ethnic or religious group, getting to know a loving and caring person from that group, someone who shatters all the stereotypes, can be liberating and disturbing at the same time. We realize that things are not what they seem.

I belabor this point about the difficulty of changing paradigms because in the discussion that follows, as I present dimensions of modern and postmodern paradigms, I do not want to simplify and domesticate these paradigms to make the paradigm shift feel safe and secure. The transition from modernity to postmodernity is anything but safe or secure. That's partly because we are in its midstream, making it difficult to map the terrain, but also because so much is at stake with the erosion and eventual disintegration of a worldview that has felt settled and secure for a long time.

Introducing Modernity

Modernity can be defined as a cluster of assumptions, beliefs, and values gathered under the banner of the Enlightenment in eighteenth-century Europe and North America. While such a definition identifies a pivotal stage in the emergence of modernity, it does not sufficiently account for Enlightenment antecedents or for the way this cluster of assumptions, beliefs, and values continues to hold sway even in the midst of a newly emerging postmodernity. Nor does this definition set forth the specific assumptions, beliefs, and values typical of modernity. In the following paragraphs I will employ typical modernist themes to illustrate modernity's origins, some of them quite old, to probe the continuing power of modernity, and to show where modernity is faltering as a postmodern paradigm takes its place.

The typical modernist themes I will discuss are these: a worldview in which humanity is the final measure of all things, not God (or religion) and not the state (or particular forms of political organization); a belief that all nature, including human nature, is governed by laws inherent in nature, laws that can be discovered and used to improve human welfare, along with the doctrine of an objectively existing and knowable universe increasingly understood by human reason and scientific discovery, leading to technologies creating a better world for all; the belief in universal human rights known by examining human nature, rights that need the protection of nations and international governance structures; the belief in inevitable progress as reason, science, and technology add to the store of human knowledge and create a better world; the belief in the autonomous self, where vision, passion, and knowledge unite in an absolute authority that must not be violated by imposed rules or customs; the belief that representative democracy is the best form of governance, since it depends on the consent of the governed; the belief that market-based capitalism is the normative theory and practice of economics since it is based on the laws of human behavior in the marketplace; and the belief that Western nations have an obligation to spread these enlightened and universal truths and practices over the globe, a belief summed up in the phrase "manifest destiny."

The Human Center

Modernity's foundations were laid in the late Middle Ages and the Renaissance in Europe, roughly the thirteenth through the sixteenth centuries C.E., when there was a rebirth of interest in and a recovery of ancient Greek and Roman philosophy, art, and architecture. Ancient and medieval theological and philosophical truths came under fresh scrutiny, with the Copernican discovery that the planets revolved about the sun, not the earth. In the arts the beauty of nature and the human body were depicted in more naturalistic ways. And in architecture the styles of Greece and Rome became favored over earlier Romanesque and Gothic models. Increasingly the right of the medieval Catholic Church to define truth was challenged as thinkers went their own way, willing to challenge official truths imposed by church or state. While the Catholic Church continued to claim authority over the state in matters of beliefs and morals, increasingly secular city-states found ways to exercise their own authority, and with the rise of cities came the beginnings of craft and trade guilds, followed by the beginnings of a middle class of privately run businesses standing outside the traditional medieval classes of the church, the nobility, and peasants. Taken all together, these changes created a new humanism, where the final measure of truth, goodness, and beauty lay not in revealed religion or in any external political authority, but in the human mind and heart. A new confidence, a new celebration of human possibilities, of the authority of human experience, took the place of submission to church and state.

Nature's Laws

Modernity also means the belief that nature, including human nature, is governed by laws laid down in the origin of the universe, and that by human observation, reason, and experimentation, these laws can be understood and used to guide human actions. This understanding of "the way things are" carries the moral obligation to act in harmony with reality, not against it. This natural law belief liberated humankind from the fear of arbitrary divine or demonic powers in the universe, which either had to be endured fatalistically or else had to be placated by the apparatus of official religion. Contrary to such fatalism, disciplines like astronomy, physics, chemistry, and biology developed out of an emerging belief in the laws of nature. Later on, human sciences — political, economic, historical, sociological, psychological, and anthropological — adopted this belief in natural laws governing human behavior, though the reality (or appearance) of human freedom continues to undermine its full grasp.

Early in modernity this lawfulness of nature and human nature was attributed to a divine creator, a religious-philosophical viewpoint called Deism. But as scientific explanations for natural phenomena were elaborated in the nineteenth and twentieth centuries, a Deistic explanation no longer seemed necessary. Whether the lawful order of nature was of divine or natural origin no longer mattered. This belief in natural laws persisted into the twentieth century and persists in the twenty-first. The actual practices of the sciences as theoretical disciplines, however, whether one looks out into space or into the inner world of atomic particles, show a universe where things are not as clearly determined as previously supposed. Degrees of apparent freedom or unpredictability appear, upsetting the theoretical apple cart, even if not undermining the predictive power of large-scale natural laws. Meanwhile the human sciences continue to struggle with the nature–nurture conflict, at the moment seeming to favor genetic and biochemical causation over societal influences. However, the overwhelming successes of applied science, in technologies of every kind, permit a degree of latitude for theoretical conundrums in the sciences. Modernity believes in the laws of nature because they work most of the time. Modernity views these natural laws as universal, not bound to particular geographies or cultures or histories. And modernity views science, technology, and the transmission of knowledge as good in and of themselves.

Universal and Inalienable Human Rights

Modernity holds that humanity is endowed by nature with rights that society must recognize and protect. These rights include life, liberty, and the pursuit of happiness, as set forth in the 1776 Declaration of Independence of the English colonies along the North American Atlantic coast. In 1789 the French National Assembly adopted its Declaration of the Rights of Man and Citizen, which listed seventeen such rights, including the affirmation that men are born and remain equal in rights, that these rights are liberty, property, security, and resistance to oppression, and that political organizations exist to protect these rights. The General Assembly of the United Nations adopted, in 1948, a Universal Declaration of Human Rights, stating, in the preamble, that the inherent dignity and the equal and unalienable rights of all members of the human family constitute the foundation of freedom, justice, and peace in the world.

However, in the eighteenth century when newly democratized nations tried to order themselves on the foundation of universal human rights, their purview was often limited, typically excluding property-less men, women, slaves, and religious or racial/ethnic minorities. The rise of nationalism in nineteenth-century Europe further compromised a belief in universal human rights. This nationalism conferred human rights by defining membership in a particular nation-state, or in a particular cultural and linguistic heritage. In her book *Inventing Human Rights,* Lynn Hunt describes how nineteenth-century nationalism and supposedly scientific racial theories justified granting rights to some but denying them to others on the basis of their genetic inferiority.[3] It was only after the horrors produced by such beliefs became clear in the wars and holocausts of the twentieth century that a revised doctrine of universal human rights was adopted by the United Nations Declaration in 1948. While this Declaration does not have formal legal standing in member states, it serves as a body of shared moral convictions guiding the way every person should be treated. In spite of an increased awareness of the diversity of human cultures, modernity continues to believe in universal human rights. Cultures that are openly sexist, racist, genocidal, or homophobic increasingly find themselves challenged by modernity's belief in universal human rights.

The Autonomous Self—Passion and Power

The rational self of the Enlightenment, freed from the authority of state or church, was still constrained by the universal order of reason in which careful observations and sound reasoning yielded universal truth. In the late eighteenth and nineteenth centuries, however, this reasoning self was gradually supplemented, or even supplanted, by the autonomous self empowered by passion. Idealism in philosophy and Romanticism in the humanities fostered this enlargement of the autonomous self. Philosophers like Schopenhauer and Nietzsche encouraged their readers to blend the passion for self-expression with the will to prevail, even by the use of forceful means. The constraints of law and custom needed to be overthrown, in this view, so that the beauty and power of individual genius could be fully expressed. Nietzsche's notion of a superior human being (*übermensch*) as a savior figure renewing human culture and history attracted romantics and rebels, but did not bring about the fundamental changes for which Nietszche hoped.

This idea of an autonomous self driven by passion and seeking to enforce its will on the world did not yield a social order based on just laws, though the fascist and state socialist regimes of the twentieth century did draw on its core beliefs. Nevertheless, even after the morally despicable practices of these regimes and their eventual collapse, the autonomous self fired with passion seeking to enforce its will is still deeply entrenched in the psyche of modernity, elevating the goal of self-fulfillment above other aims. This rebellious individualism continues to inspire modernity even if its extremes cannot be tolerated. The lonely, creative genius is as much a leading figure in modernity as is the scientist following the rules of research or the engineer who devises the technical means to employ scientific findings for human betterment.

Postmodernity: Critique and Alternative Worldviews

Postmodernity, as a term, first appeared in mid-twentieth-century writings that critically questioned the beliefs and values of modernity. During the 1960s in Western societies historians and literary critics took up the cause of groups left out or silenced in mainstream histories and lists of important writings — racial minorities, women, the poor, homosexuals, the handicapped, dissident groups outside the political or religious consensus, and others lost from sight. Scholars labored to uncover and then write alternative histories and to argue for the inclusion of new texts from these suppressed voices.

In science and philosophy new discoveries about the apparently undetermined behavior of tiny, subatomic particles or, in the vast domain of astronomy, such necessary explanatory constructs as black holes, challenged the belief that nature acted lawfully and the belief that mathematical formulas were the best representations of nature's laws. The criteria of formal beauty and elegance entered into scientific thinking. A growing awareness of diverse cultural histories and values led some to conclude that even science and mathematics are culture-specific rather than universally true. While it became clear that the uses and purposes of science are culture-specific, it was also clear that the rules of science and mathematics had achieved a high degree of universality. And in philosophy this same doubt about an objectively knowable universe, the knowledge of which could be stated with incontrovertibly true propositions, gave way to the view that, as Idealist philosophers had argued, we know the real world only with our perceptions. Objectively true knowledge is thus replaced by probable knowledge where many perceptions agree and can be composed into a coherent picture. This abandonment of universal and objective truth opened the way for diverse cultural and individual perceptions of reality and the acknowledgement that no truth claims were privileged over any other.

Postmodernity entered politics, the social sciences, and economics by way of critiques of political domination by traditional elites, typically white and male, of European ancestry and holding Western cultural beliefs and values, dominations in which diverse gender, racial, ethnic, and economically deprived groups were suppressed, ignored, or ruled out of consideration altogether. In the social sciences, any notion of a normative or ideal human nature that holds for every culture gave way to the understanding that within limits set by heredity, human nature is quite diverse in its cultural expressions, from beliefs and values all the way to the most detailed customs and habits. And in economics, the nineteenth- and twentieth-century conflict between free market economic theory, where competition was the rule, and socialist economic theory, where cooperation was the rule (each of them thoroughly modernist in the belief that their theories represented a law of nature), gave way to new realities. Economic globalization with its attendant worries about the loss of jobs and capital from rich nations to poor nations, the way wealthy nations continue to manage their economies in keeping with their national interests, and the growing economic influence of Asian nations along with the chronic economic malaise in African nations — these are all signs of a postmodern shift in economic thinking and practice, even though free market mythology continues to evoke politically conservative commitment.

While postmodernity begins with fundamental critiques of modernist assumptions and values, these critiques hint at alternative worldviews not yet fully developed into a coherent postmodern alternative. Such a recognizably postmodern alternative would, in fact, seem to be a contradiction of postmodernist affirmations about the inherent value of pluralism and diversity. In the paragraphs that follow, I will present postmodern critiques of the core assumptions and values of modernity, and with each critique identify its implicit vision for alternative viewpoints. These critical themes include the denial of any universal human nature or single human narrative, the denial of a knowable universe under the administration of universal laws, the affirmation of cultural and racial–ethnic pluralism along with diversities of gender, sexual orientation, and socioeconomic class; a decentering of the autonomous self of modernity into a self-in-community representing diverse cultural traditions, each tradition valid in its own context; and the view that knowledge is always at the service of diverse and often conflicting interests, with power rather than reason the measure of useful knowledge.

No Universal Human Nature, No Universal Human Narrative

Postmodernity challenges the modernist assumption that human beings, of whatever culture and historic period, are essentially the same, possessing a rational mind, able to perceive external reality accurately, and able to discern the truth about nature and themselves. Postmodernists doubt that education based on science can produce ever greater progress toward an objective understanding of nature and human nature. In place of any universalizing view of human nature, postmodernity offers diverse culture- and history-grounded understandings of human nature, understandings that emphasize the particular, the unique, and the local. Postmodernists do not challenge scientific descriptions of the common human gene pool or the essential biochemical constitution of each human being. But these genetic and biochemical commonalities do not warrant, according to postmodernity, claims for a universal human nature, since so much of the construction of the mind, of the social self, and of patterns of behavior are culturally and historically determined. These challenges of modernist assumptions are meant, among other things, to abolish any Western–Enlightenment presumptions about being the bearers of a universal human nature and to expose the way such modernist beliefs have been used to justify Western colonial expansion over the globe, as well as attempts to root out the cultures and religions of colonized peoples, replacing them with supposedly superior Western ways.

Postmodernity's rejection of a universal human nature also entails a rejection of any universal human narrative. That word "narrative" is a key term in understanding postmodernity. In postmodern thought, cultures, societies, and individuals create and share narratives explaining their experience. These narratives stand in the place of universal truth or objective reality as claimed in modernity. Narratives are diverse, detailed, culture-specific, and, at their best, include the narratives of marginalized and oppressed people. Modernity seeks a universal human narrative in the midst of this pluralism of narratives, while postmodernity challenges the right to impose a single narrative on the complex diversities of cultures and their histories. Twentieth-century "world history" textbooks in the West, for example, began with brief references to Egyptian and Mesopotamian cultures, but hurried on to ancient Greece and Rome, then Europe, and finally the United States — a universal narrative that, alas, left much out and created false impressions of superiority and inferiority. Postmodernity insists on preserving and studying many narratives, particularly the narratives of the excluded — women, the poor, racial-ethnic minorities, and people of diverse sexual orientations.

These postmodern rejections of any single doctrine of humankind or common human narrative raise profoundly troubling questions about the possibility of any cross-cultural communication or community formation, particularly if participants act as if their own heritage is normative for all humanity. Diverse interests and unequal powers come into play. Who wins and who loses — those with wealth and the coercive power of the state over the poor and powerless? Clearly the search for the "commonly human" must begin with mutual respect. But how to move beyond that? Richard Rorty, a postmodernist philosopher, argued that a pragmatic test of every proposal in light of its promise to enhance freedom, dignity, and well-being would be a sufficient measure of truth and value. But does such a proposal repeat the fallacy of a universalizing narrative?

No Objective Reality,
No Universal Laws of Nature

These denials by postmodernity may seem an absurd contradiction of common sense. Everyone knows there is a real world out there and that it has its rules that must be learned and honored. Gravity seems to work the same in Zimbabwe as it does in Germany. Postmodernity, however, is not so fanciful as to believe that since all knowledge is a product of social construction, reality is what anyone says it is. Reality is always established by a process of intersubjective validation, not by some correspondence between a logical argument or mathematical formula with a piece of reality as modernity would have it. Intersubjective validation means a process of reflection on experience where varying degrees of probability are discerned about the way the world works. This could sound like a majority vote, but that overly simplifies an ongoing and highly complex process. Some of these probabilities, like Newtonian mechanics, do not require explicit intersubjective validation, but are simply taken for granted, which is common sense. Other matters, however, like the value and purpose of human life, require both claims about what is objectively real and also the claims of tradition, history, and culture. Living with varying degrees of probability may seem unacceptable in the context of the firm modernist conviction that there is a knowable, objective reality. But degrees of probability are all we have, postmodernists contend, and we must make the best of it. Imperial objective truth has been dethroned; in its place rules the best socially constructed truth we can imagine.

The laws of nature fall under these same strictures in postmodern thought. While there are observable regularities in nature and human history, these regularities disclose varying degrees of probability. The hope that more precise research will refine our grasp of nature's laws and our ability to predict and control outcomes, as imagined by modernists, is doomed to fail both epistemologically and morally, as questions of who has the right to manipulate and control nature's processes become urgent. Tucked into this dilemma is the modernist belief that since scientists know more, their views should carry more weight than the views of politicians or the people. Postmodernity would argue for rules of discourse that value scientific knowledge without privileging science above other ways of knowing.

These postmodern denials of an objectively knowable world and of laws of nature may seem perverse and even silly to one who is firmly grounded in modernity. But there are important affirmations underneath these denials, which can be summed up this way: Reality is perceived and known in the context of diverse cultural traditions and histories. It is vitally important that all these diverse perceptions and the traditions in which they are grounded be accorded respect and not rejected out of hand when they seem to clash with modernist convictions. Though it would seem wasteful to reopen the question of whether the earth is round or flat, or if there is a common human genome, there is value in exploring less settled questions, such as, whether nature discloses an intelligence guiding its evolution. If diverse cultures and their histories can share equally and respectfully in a quest for the kind of shared reality that embraces many differing features, not pressing for a universal law of everything, then a better human prospect and improved prospects for nature might emerge. Most postmodernists, I would guess, believe in such a hope and method, but would acknowledge that little progress has been made in its implementation, and little progress can occur until dominating modernist views of reality and nature's laws can be set aside.

Pluralism and Diversity Affirmed; Hierarchies Rejected

As postmodernity rejects an objectively knowable nature and its natural laws, postmodernity also affirms the principle of pluralism and diversity, where hierarchies are to be rejected. This principle means that diverse cultures and their histories are to be cherished and affirmed, not arranged in any kind of hierarchy of value or truth but encouraged to pursue their own development according to their inherent values. The resulting diversity is prized because it enriches the world and adds to its interest. Diversity is affirmed because it better represents the realities of the world of nature and the human place in that nature. Any hierarchy of value — philosophies that seek the most unifying and abstract understanding of being itself; political systems that value the concentration of power and the use of violence by the few against the welfare of all; economic systems that concentrate wealth and power in the hands of the few while many live in poverty; systemic racism, sexism, homophobia, and classism that deny full human dignity and opportunity to many — all such hierarchies are to be rejected in favor of radical equality and justice for all. Postmodernity also rejects any hierarchy in the arts and humanities. Distinctions between popular culture and high culture, or serious and frivolous arts are rejected. Every cultural expression is of equal value to its creators and users and of equal value in understanding the spirit of the times.

The Autonomous Self Decentered; Self in Community

Postmodernity challenges the cherished modernist idea of an autonomous self, governed by reason, in an Enlightenment way of thinking, or by the passion for self-awareness and self-realization characterizing Romanticism. Postmodernity proposes that in the place of the autonomous self, the idea of self-in-community is both a more accurate depiction of the self and also a more fruitful pathway to a humane social order. The notion that the self is socially constructed is not new and not an invention of postmodernity. George Herbert Mead, pioneering social psychologist; Sigmund Freud, founder of psychoanalysis; and B. F. Skinner, the behaviorist, understood the self as socially constructed. What they made of that fact, however, was within a modernist worldview — the belief that enhanced self-awareness about the social construction of the self would liberate the self, giving it more control over its destiny. Against that belief, postmodernists argue that the idea of self-in-community promises no such enhanced autonomy, but does promise a sense of self where the typically modern agonies of anomie, isolation, and loneliness are overcome in the reality of self-in-community, a self that is centered enough to allow a continuing exchange between self and community in which both are enriched. This de-centering of the autonomous self may alarm modernists who see the power of choice reduced or lost altogether in postmodernity. But the autonomous self, like the ostensibly autonomous voluntary association, may be more illusory than actual.

How the United Church of Christ Became Enmeshed in Modernity

With these sketches of modernist and postmodern themes in mind, and mindful of the disorienting perils of this present time of transition from modernity to postmodernity in Western cultures, I turn now to a description of how the United Church of Christ, especially its ecclesiology and polity, became so enmeshed in modernity and remains ill-suited to postmodernity.

First, though, I need to define ecclesiology and polity again and then describe the functions of ecclesiology and polity in the United Church of Christ. Ecclesiology is the doctrine of the church, or the way the church is understood theologically. Polity is the way the church is organized to carry out its mission, or the ways in which the organization is governed. Many in the United Church of Christ, I would guess (and perhaps many people in other traditions), would question whether God gives the church as part of the gift of the gospel, in other words, whether God intended for there to be churches as we know them. While Jesus called disciples, it is not clear from the gospels that he intended for them, and new followers, to become churches. In spite of these important questions, the witness of the Christian heritage attests that being called into community and affirming that call is intrinsic to the gift of the gospel itself. That means, therefore, the church is not an optional response of faith — it is requirement. That is precisely what ecclesiology means.

Polity defines governance and authority in church organizations. Historically in Western churches, councils, bishops, synods, and local churches shared governance, along with secular rulers and parliaments. The Protestant Reformation ancestor churches of the United Church of Christ — primarily Reformed and Free Church bodies — believed that the scriptures revealed God's design for church organization, as well as setting forth the gospel message. This design was created from New Testament books describing early church life. From this heritage the United Church of Christ has viewed its polity as an essential aspect of its identity. Thus polity has become an article of faith, taking on an ecclesiological tone. It's not that "they will know we are Christians by our love" but that they will know we are UCC Christians by our polity. In the time just before the union in 1957, and immediately afterward, this polity was characterized as autonomous bodies (local churches, associations, conferences, the national setting) relating to one another responsibly. Since the Constitutional revisions of 2000, the official phrase has been a "polity of covenant," with all the biblical and theological connotations of the word "covenant."

The ecclesiology of the United Church of Christ is not so readily grasped in a single phrase, however. Founding documents like the Basis of Union, the Constitution, and the Statement of Faith affirm the ancient ecumenical creeds, where ecclesiology was expressed compactly as "one holy catholic and apostolic church," a rich phrase but not very specific. Protestant Reformers stressed the validity of word and sacrament as marks of the true church. They believed that the church is composed of all those who confess Jesus Christ as Son of God and Savior, and the belief that Jesus Christ is the sole head of the church. The UCC Statement of Faith sets forth a fuller ecclesiology in its confession that the Holy Spirit is the one who calls the church into being and in its list of the attributes of church life — discipleship, service, proclamation, resistance, and membership in Christ at the font and table, along with identification with his passion and victory.

But when UCC church leaders wrestled in the 1960s and 1970s with unresolved polity issues, particularly how endowed boards with histories of independent action would relate to the General Synod and denominational officers, Avery Post, then President of the UCC, and other national leaders began to speak of an "ecclesiological deficit" that needed to be addressed. These leaders believed that ecclesiology should shape polity decisions, rather than tradition, inertia, or power politics. This lack of ecclesiological attention was keenly felt by UCC representatives to ecumenical conversations, where representatives from other churches wondered whether the UCC was really a church, as its name suggests, or merely an assemblage of churches with no clear center or boundaries. Louis Gunnemann, in *United and Uniting,* lamented this ecclesiological confusion that turned up in ecumenical efforts in which the UCC was engaged at the time when he wrote.[4] In the 1990s, the General Synod appointed a Committee on Structures to recommend organizational changes for the national setting of the church. A subcommittee on ecclesiology was part of its design, in the hope that this ecclesiological deficit could be addressed. The work of the subcommittee, and then the entire Committee on Structures, showed that a unified statement of UCC ecclesiology, like the parallel polity phrase, "a polity of covenant," was not possible. The Committee on Structures presented two documents as part of its report, "United Church of Christ Ecclesiology," and "A Mission Framework for the General Synod Committee on Structure." While not contradicting each other, these two documents accent differing ecclesiological themes: the founding Christological ecclesiology, and viewing the church as engaged in the mission of God. There are, in fact, two other ecclesiological themes presently affirmed in the UCC: (1) The church as communities/organizations living together in covenant relations, as understood biblically and theologically; and (2) the church as a radically welcoming community listening to the still-speaking God.

How serious is this remaining ecclesiological diversity and confusion? Some might argue that the phrase "covenant relations" says everything that needs to be said in both ecclesiology and polity. But that would perpetuate confusion over ecclesiology and polity. At the time of this writing, though, the phrase "covenantal relations" seems to suffice for both ecclesiology and polity. Thus ecclesiology is allowed to be theologically diverse, as with other theological topics. The polity of covenant relations, however, does not allow for commensurate diversity. This polity understanding is, after all, a product of the hopes of the UCC founders to create a church with a new kind of polity that is neither absolute congregationalism nor absolute presbyterianism. And if everyone clearly understood what covenant means biblically and theologically, covenant might suffice ecclesiologically as well. But everyone does not seem to understand it that way. In practice covenantal relations are taken to mean that all parts of the church should consult with all other parts of the church before acting unilaterally. But when that does not work, what then? Patience, prayer, and persuasion are the only recourse. There are no generally accepted consequences for a failure to honor covenant relations, however egregious these failures might be. The oversight of clergy and other authorized ministers as spelled out in the *Manual on Ministry* is the notable exception: association committees on the ministry using the *Manual* have the authority to remove authorized ministerial standing, though local settings of ministry are still legally free to employ such persons in ministerial roles if they choose not to honor the covenant. Here then is one aspect of UCC polity practice has consequences for covenant-breaking, but other aspects do not.

In either ecclesiological or polity discussions, however, when biblical covenants are invoked — God with Israel, with all of creation in Jesus Christ, and with the church in the power of the Holy Spirit — it is no longer a matter of equal parties consulting about a good outcome. Biblically and theologically it is the initiating grace of the living God that makes covenants with promises and warnings, blessings if covenants are kept, punishments if they are not. While some UCC believers may hold such a quid-pro-quo view of God, most would not, lest divine grace could be earned by good works, a view decisively rejected in the

Pauline, Augustinian, and Reformation traditions at the heart of the UCC heritage.

These distortions of covenantal definitions of ecclesiology and polity in the United Church of Christ are good examples of the entanglement of the church with modernity. The modernist belief in autonomy — the autonomous self, or the autonomous local church in relation to autonomous regional or national church expressions — is taken for granted in UCC polity practices. And though covenantal commitments are understood to mean an obligation to consult and arrive at mutually affirmed decisions, when time runs out and patience falters, a vote is taken, the winners take all, and the losers sulk or leave. Autonomy trumps covenant every time. Such decisions can be as local as an individual or family choosing to leave a local church, or a local church choosing to leave the denomination; or such decisions can be as denomination-wide as a vote by covenanted ministries boards to oppose restructuring proposals on the grounds of perceived threats to the autonomous boards' mission mandates.

Protestant Reformation Foundations of Modernity

The ecclesiological and polity foundations of the United Church of Christ were laid in the late sixteenth and early seventeenth centuries, during the English and Swiss reformations. Each of these movements followed Calvin's prescriptions for reforming the church more than Luther's. But they eventually took different paths depending on their respective political settings.

In England the monarchy played a critical role in the Reformation, with the king, Henry VIII, and later queen Elizabeth I officially heading the Church of England. English Calvinists advocated a more thorough reformation of the church along Swiss lines. But the Queen preferred a moderate course of reform, stressing national unity and loyalty to the monarch. These Calvinist English Reformers were called Puritans because they sought to purify the Church of England of its persisting medieval Catholic practices.

Two Puritan factions emerged from this struggle: those advocating a presbyterian form of church governance as in Calvin's Geneva, with the support of the state, and those advocating a separation of Reformed churches from ecclesiastical and secular rule. These Separatists, or Independents, as they came to be called, were persecuted, their leaders arrested and in some instances executed, with others fleeing to Holland. From these religious émigrés came the Pilgrims who sailed on the *Mayflower* to establish, in 1620, the Plymouth Bay Colony in New England.

These Separatist Puritans declared that Jesus Christ is the sole head of the church, a principle affirmed in the history of Congregationalism and appearing in the Preamble to the Constitution of the United Church of Christ. To understand the meaning of this affirmation in the UCC nowadays we need to recall its sixteenth- and seventeenth-century meanings. The sole headship of Jesus Christ was first of all a critical principle. It meant that no secular power — monarch, parliament, magistrates, congress, or president — had any authority to exercise rule in the church or over the church. And there was a second critical principle: no ecclesiastical power outside the gathered community of Christian believers — popes, bishops, councils, synods, assemblies, or church executives — had any authority over the local church. This rejection of outside ecclesiastical authority did not mean, however, that such wider church entities and relationships were of no use. The principle of consultation among churches, given its classical formulation in the New England Cambridge Platform of 1648, affirmed the value of synods, assemblies, associations, and other such relationships, so long as it was clearly understood that these were consultations relying on prayerful persuasion, not authorities compelling assent. Congregationalism has held to this principle across the years, though not always to its practice.

These two critical functions of belief in the sole headship of Jesus Christ in the church do not tell the whole story, however, nor do they explicate the fuller ecclesiological implications of this confession. The positive affirmations are these: Every gathered congregation possesses everything it needs to be fully the church — the Word of God, in the scriptural, preaching, and doctrinal senses; and the sacraments of baptism and holy communion, authorized by their fidelity to the Word, needing no wider ecclesiastical authorization such as ordination or approval by a bishop or an assembly. Following the theological lead of Calvin, these Congregationalists also affirmed a belief in the real presence of Jesus Christ in the preaching of the Word and in the sacramental observances of communion and baptism. This was a spiritual presence, not couched in the medieval and ancient vocabulary of substances, a term that framed the Catholic-Lutheran debate over Christ's presence in the Eucharistic bread and wine. But even though it was a spiritual presence, it was a real presence, nonetheless.

The Swiss reformation, inaugurated by Zwingli in Zurich in 1522, but more fully developed in Geneva by Calvin, beginning in 1541, did not declare that Jesus Christ is sole head of the church in the same way as did the Puritan Separatists in England. Calvin's ecclesiology did affirm the primacy of Word and Sacrament as defining the true church, though he also stressed the doctrine of election in identifying those in heaven and on earth who comprised the church. Calvin also emphasized the preaching and teaching of sound doctrine as a mark of the church. While Calvin's Reformed ecclesiology shared the English Separatist rejection of ecclesiastical authority as practiced in the Roman Catholic tradition, it did hold that the secular rulers (in Calvin's case the magistrates of Geneva) were obligated to support and protect the church and to punish heretics who refused to recant. Calvin argued that the offices of pastor, elder, teacher, and deacon were biblically established for leading the church, and that secular magistrates were to follow the teachings of church elders or presbyters. From Geneva came presbyterial church polity, which means that the assembly of the elders, or presbytery, governs the churches in its region of responsibility, including the formation and ordination of elders, and decisions about church doctrines, discipline, and other matters.

My purpose in going over the beginnings of these two ecclesiological and polity traditions foundational to the United Church of Christ is to show how their Reformation outlook gradually opened to modernity and then embraced modernity. It is tempting to say that it was all Calvin's fault, since his theology framed the faith traditions of English Puritans as well as Swiss, German, French, Dutch, and Scottish Reformed and Presbyterians churches. In his book *A Secular Age*, Charles Taylor leans that way. He speaks of Calvinism's "long-term contribution to the rise of humanism. This came about precisely through the drive to re-order society, not only in its church structure, but in its secular life as well."[5] This Calvinist ordering of secular society, developed first in Geneva, then in the Massachusetts Bay Colony and in England during Cromwell's rule, had the effect, Taylor is saying, of encouraging the emergence of what he calls "exclusive humanism" in Western civilization, by which he means a humanism drained of its divine foundation. This draining process required many centuries, Taylor believes, as reform movements become linked to Enlightenment values and then revolutionary political philosophies.

For my purpose, we need not pursue Taylor's analysis in detail, but we should note that Calvinism's doctrinal orthodoxy, especially the doctrines of election and predestination, along with its disciplined personal and social morality enforced by both church and state, eventually do weaken and in modernity virtually disappear. In the place of Calvinist doctrine and church/state practices, modern enlightened political philosophies provide beliefs and values supporting the idea of a just social order, one that protects the freedom and rights of its members.

Modernity Embedded: The Nineteenth Century

The path taken by New England Congregationalism and the German Reformed Church in the United States, the Calvinist forebears of United Church of Christ ecclesiology and polity, are sufficiently different to justify describing them separately. But in spite of those differences, they come out at nearly the same place in the present-day life of the United Church of Christ.

In New England Congregationalism two modernist values prevailed: (1) the autonomy of the local church (with the autonomy of individual conscience assumed but never stated) and (2) the church's calling to be a progressive influence in society. For the German Reformed Church the dominant modernist value was due process, a kind of lingering Presbyterianism of the spirit if not the law.

The further modernizing of Congregationalism in the nineteenth century involved the development of an American liberal theology as an alternative to strict Calvinist beliefs, an emphasis on religious growth as more natural and proper than a revivalist conversion, as well as the search for ways to accommodate new science-based theories about origins (Darwin), social and economic development (Marx), and psychological development (Freud). These modernizing theological developments went hand in hand with Congregationalist efforts to abolish slavery, to establish missions in the West and on other continents, and at the end of the century to embrace the Social Gospel as a response to the evils of industrialization.

These themes appear in both the Burial Hill Declaration of 1865 and the Kansas City Statement of Faith of 1913,[6] statements adopted at meetings of the National Council of Congregational Churches. While both statements contain brief traditional confessions of faith in the triune God, their modernizing trajectories are clear in statements like these: Burial Hill — "its [Congregationalism's] principles to elevate society, to regulate education, to civilize humanity, to purify law, to reform the Church and the State, and to assert and defend liberty"; and as expressed at Kansas City, "We hold it to be the mission of the Church of Christ to proclaim the Gospel to all mankind, exalting the worship of the one true God, and laboring for the progress of knowledge, the promotion of justice, the reign of peace, and the realization of human brotherhood." While I do not mean to suggest that the traditional confessions of faith in these declarations were a mere formality, I do believe that the weight in the passages just quoted demonstrates a shift from faith as personal and communal belief to faith as action in society to promote human welfare. It is no wonder that this Congregationalist commitment to progressive social influence should carry over into the United Church of Christ with its current commitment to be a "multiracial, multicultural, just peace, open and affirming, and accessible to all" denomination.

The modernist legacy of the German Reformed Church (later the Reformed Church in the United States and finally the Evangelical and Reformed Church after the merger of 1934) appears in what I called earlier its commitment to due process, or to preserving the spirit of presbyterial church order if not its legally binding character. This commitment led eighteenth-century German Reformed settlers in the American colonies at first to relate to the Dutch Reformed Church in New York and then in Holland for proper ecclesial and pastoral support. Eventually German Reformed people in the newly independent United States of America created their own denominational structures, first through its *Coetus* of clergy organized in 1747, which then was dissolved in 1793 with the formation of the first Synod of the German Reformed Church in the United States of America. Regional groups of churches were organized as part of that polity process. Along with these denominationally formative polity structures came the organization of the first seminary, colleges, and missionary associations.

Theologically and liturgically the German Reformed Church was anchored by the *Heidelberg Catechism* and the Palatinate Liturgy. The Catechism was thoroughly Calvinist in its doctrinal substance, but with a focus on the blessings of faithful obedience that gave it a pious and irenic tone, making it less a document of dispute than were other Reformed confessions, like the Helvetic, Dort, or Westminster Confessions. And the Palatinate Liturgy maintained the essential form of Calvinist worship, with emphasis on preaching, sound teaching, and free prayer. Therefore early German Reformed settlers in America were not as preoccupied as New England Congregationalists over defining the church and its polity, nor were they as divided over the first waves of theological liberalism and the First Great Awakening as were Congregationalists. But a time of testing soon came upon the German Reformed

Church. The revivals of the Second Great Awakening (1800–1830s) initiated disputes in the German Reformed Church, as in other denominations, over how extensively revivalism's "new measures" should be allowed into the church. One new measure was the anxious bench, a seat in the front of the church where people troubled in their conscience by sin and guilt might kneel in prayer surrounded by the faithful — deacons or other church leaders — who would place their hands on the heads of the penitents and seek to "pray them" into conversion, where the penitents confessed, repented, and then were raised to a new and holy life. Early in the Second Awakening German Reformed pastors cautiously supported the revivals, but were troubled by their excesses — excessive emotional displays with sudden conversions, and the number if itinerant revival preachers who were unlearned and preached unauthorized by any church.

At the German Reformed seminary at Mercersburg Professors Nevin and Schaff led the movement to create a new Reformed ecclesiology reaching back to the ancient confessional marks of the church, holding that the true church is one, holy, catholic, and apostolic. Their reforms were both ecclesial and liturgical. Conflicts raged between the Mercersburg and Old Reformed parties over liturgical practices and ecclesiological beliefs that divided the German Reformed Church for many years. The Mercersburg party favored an ancient, classical ecclesial doctrine, purged of its later Roman Catholic distortions, and advocated liturgical worship centered on the altar and the sacraments rather than preaching and free prayers. The Old Reformed party opposed the Mercersburg reforms and defended traditional Calvinist preaching, doctrine, and simple worship. The Directory of Worship of 1887 attempted to blend Mercersburg and Old Reformed liturgical practices, but it never attained widespread use, according to David Dunn.[7] Dunn also describes how this protracted conflict over worship came to represent polity differences in the German Reformed Church, with the Mercersburg party emphasizing the authority of the Synod over classis and congregation, while the Old Reformed party stressed the autonomy of the local church over its own worship practices.

Throughout all these conflicts, the German Reformed Church discussed, debated, and voted on the contentious ecclesiological and liturgical issues with a seriousness and persistence characteristic of its heritage. They believed that properly chosen delegates from the churches were authorized to wrestle with these difficult matters, and eventually to decide the outcome.

This Mercersburg story might seem a needless detour in my exposition of Reformed contributions to a modernist ecclesiology and polity in the United Church of Christ, but I want to show how a modernist commitment to due process, or a presbyterianism of the spirit if not of law, persists in the United Church of Christ, and how it appeared in the union negotiations as well as in denominational life after 1957, particularly in the Constitutional revisions of 2000. To do that, I need to go back to the debates over the Interpretations of the Basis of Union in 1948, where, in Gunnemann's narrative, the commitment of the Evangelical and Reformed Church to union and to creating a new kind of church and new polity was stronger than in the Congregational and Christian denomination, where protecting local autonomy and freedom was stronger than its ecumenical impulse.[8] Clearly, for the sake of union, the Evangelical and Reformed Church did give up its presbyterial polity for an as yet undefined new polity, one that would be something new, not just Congregationalism continuing unaffected. This Reformed commitment to due process persisted after the union of 1957. Evangelical and Reformed leaders in the new church led the way in persistently calling for due process in working out the implications of the new UCC polity. Gunnemann himself was one of those advocates. In his writings and speeches he challenged the United Church of Christ to be faithful to its Constitutional provisions for autonomous congregations and other entities relating to one another responsibly, in covenant relations. Gunnemann was not alone in identifying the new polity as one of covenant. Others took up the concept as well. As the *Manual on Ministry* became a more comprehensive guidebook to polity and ministerial practices in the UCC, its language became the language of covenant. Eventually the language of covenant appeared in the Constitutional revisions of 2000, with a new Constitutional Article III describing covenant relations. The concept of covenant relations now stands, I am suggesting, as an enduring legacy of German Reformed presbyterial polity.

In the previous chapter I questioned whether the biblical and theological language of covenant employed to describe UCC polity had really accomplished more than adding a greater awareness that free, autonomous bodies in the United Church of Christ — principally local churches, but including other expressions of the church — are obligated to consult with one another. Setting that question aside for the moment, I do want to argue that the heritage of German Reformed presbyterial polity, as illustrated earlier in the Mercersburg debates and as illustrated in concerns about the Interpretations of the Basis of Union of 1948, and then in the evolving polity practice and terminology of covenant from 1957 to 2000, has profoundly shaped a polity reflecting the assumptions and values of modernity.

It would not be fair to other ecclesial streams flowing into the United Church of Christ to pass over their contributions to ecclesiology or polity. The Evangelical Synod of the West, the Christian Connection churches, the German Congregational churches, and other bodies from national or racial/ethnic traditions have made significant contributions. But my purpose here is not to trace and sort out all their unique legacies, but to focus on those two Calvinist/Reformed streams that, in my view, have most strongly influenced the creation of an ecclesiology and polity embedded in modernity.

In the paragraphs that follow, then, I will focus and summarize the modernist heritage from these two streams of Reformed ecclesiology and polity just described, New England Congregationalism and the German Reformed Church.

Autonomy: Self and Local Church

The New England Congregationalist commitment to autonomy, formally the autonomy of the local congregation but by implication always the autonomy of the individual conscience, reveals a thoroughly modernist outlook. Believing that the enlightened individual conscience, or that the informed local congregation, have everything needed to be faithful congregations, to make sound and reasonable decisions, that truth and value are local and that bad things happen when local autonomy is compromised by bureaucratic entanglements — these are all expression of modernity's unquestioned assumptions. Allied with these expressions are modernist assumptions about reason and experience, about natural law, about inalienable human rights, and about the progressive character of human history.

In postmodernity it is becoming increasingly clear that the autonomous self is no such thing, but a complex network of influences, often at war with one another and often acting unreasonably. In postmodernity it is becoming increasingly clear that the local church, or any other local institution, is at the mercy of the forces of marketing and consumption, the politics of hate and violence as well as the politics of reason and restraint, conflicting and unresolvable priorities for the use of scarce resources between the claims of the rich and the poor, the decay of progressive institutions such as education and health care, and the erosion of any national or international political will to protect the environment — these and many other examples reveal the inadequacy of modernist assumptions and values about the autonomous self and the autonomous local church. Nevertheless in the United Church of Christ we cling to these values and assumptions in our ecclesiology and polity as though these were at the heart of our faith.

Progressive Social Influence

New England Congregationalism retained its Calvinist sense of responsibility for the well-being of society, even as it moved through theological and political transitions from Westminster Calvinism to progressive politics and liberal theology, and as it became a voluntary association in a religiously pluralistic society. A list of UCC "firsts" appears on the denominational website (*www.ucc.org*), citing early experiments in democracy (Massachusetts Bay colony), early condemnation of slavery (Samuel Sewell, 1700), the first ordained African American pastor (Lemuel Haynes, 1785), the first integrated anti-slavery society (the American Missionary Association, 1846), the first ordained woman (Antoinette Brown, 1853), and the emergence of the Social Gospel (1897) as examples of what I have called Congregationalism's legacy of progressive social influence. Many more instances could be named. They all represent a heritage of official church establishment (Colonial New England, Calvin's Geneva) that continues to assume that even in a constitutionally religiously neutral nation, it is both the right and duty of the church to labor for the improvement of society. This Congregationalist ethos, however, was one of social influence through its clergy and members, not through direct institutional action. Congregationalist philanthropists and clergy founded missionary associations and boards as well as colleges and theological schools. There were, as yet, no national denominational agencies to undertake such missions, nor would it have even occurred to early nineteenth-century Congregationalists to try that approach. They were accustomed, as were Presbyterians, Episcopalians, and Methodists, to thinking of themselves as moral teachers and exemplars for the whole society. Congregationalists were leaders in politics, business, education, and the professions almost as a matter of entitlement.

These established church values and practices, along with Congregationalists' religiously grounded opposition to slavery and then efforts to educate freed slaves, or their advocacy of the Social Gospel to address the poverty and oppression that accompanied the industrialization and urbanization of American society, led Congregationalists to advocate progressive ideologies and politics. Some even looked to socialism or communism as political and economic systems that would distribute wealth more equitably. This became an ideological clash within Congregationalism where its establishment ethos caused leading clergy and laity to defend free-market capitalism against any hint of socialism. In the 1930s and 1940s the Social Action Council of the Congregational and Christian denomination became a lightning rod for anti-socialist and anti-communist viewpoints. Those were decades when many Congregationalists were theologically liberal and politically conservative.

This Congregationalist ethos of establishment, with its obligation to guide society morally, was embraced in the United Church of Christ, but became transformed, during and following the social upheavals of the 1960s, into increasingly liberal or radical stands on social justice issues such as race, the place of women, war and nuclear arms, abortion, homosexuality, and the protection of the environment. The commitment to be a multiracial, multicultural, peace with justice, open and affirming, and accessible-to-all church sums up these religious and moral affirmations that the UCC holds up before the world. The continuing historic Congregationalist establishment ethos carried over into the UCC, however, has befuddled those accustomed to power and influence as the denomination has been increasingly edged to the political and ecclesial sidelines. Society does not listen or pay much attention anymore, not just to the United Church of Christ, but to all the old-line denominations. Militant Christian evangelicals are in the media spotlight and courted by conservative politicians. Meanwhile the old-line or formerly mainline churches anguish over their waning social influence. The graying of the mainlines, the resulting loss of members and money, the rise of militant evangelicalism, and the rightward direction of American politics around the turn of the twenty-first century are surely all factors in this unaccustomed loss of influence. What to do? — market the message more effectively, shape the message into a more centrist or main-stream mold, raise a ruckus that will attract media attention, or challenge clergy and laity to give more and do more — all these strategies will not, I fear, restore the UCC or other main-lines to positions of social influence, because all of them rely on typically modernist assumptions. They all fail to take account of postmodernity.

Reformed Due Process

The synodical system of governance created by the German Reformed Church in the United States, with regional synods of churches and a General Synod, reflected faithful adherence to a Reformed ecclesiology and polity, but without the political control exercised in Geneva or Puritan New England. This system was thoroughly presbyterial in its constitutional foundations and practice. Synodical acts mandated compliance by local churches. The same was true for the General Synod. Examining the nineteenth-century conflict over revivalism and then the Mercersburg controversy, protracted disputes over the very meaning of Reformed theology and worship, one is struck by the way the deliberative bodies — local church consistories, classes, synods, and the General Synod — took seriously their obligations to act within the constitutionally defined frameworks of their church. Gunnemann's reference to the "churchly pietism" of the German Reformed Church is certainly displayed in the minutes of these meetings, in the speeches given, and in the correspondence addressing the issues in dispute. It was finally not up to the individual believer's conscience or to the local church to decide these matters. The whole church, through its defined processes of discussion and voting, was believed to be charged with discerning the will of God, the mind of Jesus Christ, all within the leading of the Holy Spirit.

When the Reformed Church in the United States and the Evangelical Synod united in 1934, forming the Evangelical and Reformed Church, the ecumenical commitment and the sense of common heritage were strong enough to overcome worries about how a more centralized synodical polity of the Evangelicals might be blended with a presbyterial representative system. The Constitution of 1938 settled these questions, by creating a plan of government "described as essentially presbyterian but functionally congregationalist," in the words of historian Carl E. Schneider.[9] Clearly polity did not occupy a central place in the Evangelical and Reformed union, when compared with the intense negotiations during the formation of the United Church of Christ.

When the Congregational Christian General Council in 1948 adopted its Interpretations of the Basis of Union, Interpretations that guaranteed local church autonomy, it became clear that the congregational/synodical polity of the Evangelical and Reformed Church could not survive in the new United Church of Christ. Louis Gunnemann described the anxiety and frustrations of these times, when the hope for some new form of church government seemed constrained by the insistence on protecting local church autonomy.[10] The Constitution, adopted in 1961, protected local church autonomy in Paragraph 15 (now 18), but surrounded that paragraph with admonitions to keep in responsible relations with all expressions of the church, and to receive and honor actions by the General Synod, conferences, and associations.

The uniting denominations took both these protections and admonitions seriously, but with differing accents. Congregationalists prized the protections but honored the admonitions. Evangelical and Reformed people, especially from the Reformed side, acknowledged the protections but pressed for honoring the admonitions. It was from this difference that an emphasis on due process gradually took center stage in UCC ecclesial and polity developments, with the concept of covenant relations providing biblical and theological warrants for taking admonitions seriously.

My impression from my participation in the wider church during its first fifty years is that many of the voices calling for honoring covenantal relations have come from the former Evangelical and Reformed side, especially the Reformed. If I may put it a bit whimsically and with exaggeration, it's as though the Reformed have said, "All right, we gave up our polity for the sake of greater unity. But now we're going to hold you Congregationalists to those Constitutional admonitions about covenant and not let you get comfortably settled in the local church autonomy of Paragraph 18." As a result due process has become increasingly a matter of orthodox belief in the United Church of Christ, but always couched in the language of covenant relations.

I do not mean to ignore or discount the substantial contributions of New England Puritanism or its European ancestors to covenantal theology. United Church of Christ historians like Douglas Horton, Barbara Brown Zikmund, John von Rohr, and Elizabeth Nordbeck have drawn on this heritage. But I do not detect much Puritan or Reformed theological influence in the way we use the concept of covenant relations or try to practice them in the United Church of Christ today.

A case in point is the draft document *Manual on Church,* prepared and circulated by the Parish Life and Leadership Team in Local Church Ministries, one of the national UCC covenanted ministries. Draft 2, dated January 1, 2005, opens its ecclesiological discussion by affirming that Jesus Christ is the sole head of the church (lines 136–37), then noting the Reformation marks of the true church in Word and Sacraments (140–41), and concluding with the affirmation that carrying out the mission of God is the church's reason for being (143). Three ecclesiological themes follow this introduction — "beloved community, seeking justice, and engaged in God's mission." The idea of beloved community might be fruitful for a deeper ecclesiological exploration of the inner life of the church — worship and sacraments, education and catechesis, prayer and spiritual life, compassionate service to those in need — but this draft document identifies the beloved community as one engaged in the "struggle for justice, reconciliation, and liberation."

While there are references to the UCC Statement of Faith language about the cost and joy of discipleship, the governing theme of this document becomes the definition and explication of covenantal relations — among local churches, local churches with associations and conferences, and with the General Synod and its covenanted ministries. The moral and spiritual content of the mission of the church are scarcely developed, when compared with the document's admonitions on covenant relations. Especially in the discussion of the relation of autonomy to covenant relations, the notion of self-rule, which is the fundamental definition of autonomy, is reframed as the notion of autonomy as "the capacity for covenant." This is hardly the definition of autonomy emerging from Separatist and Puritan beliefs about the church and enshrined in Paragraph 18 of the Constitution. But it does represent mainstream UCC thinking about the centrality of covenant relations in defining its ecclesiology and polity.

To summarize, I have been describing how a Reformed or Calvinist ecclesiological and polity heritage has been woven into the United Church of Christ by its passage through modernity, carrying along assumptions and values from modernity that have become normative, while in the same historical process the UCC has increasingly embraced diversity and liberality in matters of faith and worship. Beliefs about autonomy, about the church as moral teacher and guide for society, and about following due process have been the main carriers of modernist assumptions and values, and, in becoming UCC orthodoxy, have rendered the denomination ill-suited to understand postmodernity and unsure about how to pursue its mission in such a new world. While that mission has clearly stated aims — seeking justice, engaging in God's mission, struggling for justice, reconciliation, and liberation — any steps toward achieving those missional aims have become tangled in the web of modernity.

These modernist assumptions and values include the belief in the autonomous individual conscience and local church as sufficient unto themselves (a procedural residue from the Reformation conviction that Jesus Christ is the sole head of the church); a belief in reasoned persuasion and education as proper ways to enlist passionate commitment to mission; the belief that due process, defined as covenantal relations, is the only way for the church to deliberate and make decisions, thus patterning the church's decision-making after Western democratic ways; a belief that progress is inevitable since the accumulation of scientific knowledge will guide decisions about its use; a belief that advanced and enlightened Western nations have both the right and duty to show the rest of the world how to become enlightened through following Western political and economic values; and with that duty, the right of Western religious institutions to watch over and influence morality to advance the progress of goodness. While the United Church of Christ has renounced Western hegemony, to its credit, it still acts as though the UCC (along with other Western churches) is entitled to call society to act justly, and then the church often seems baffled and frustrated when this call is unnoticed and unheeded. This present state of affairs is one in which a commitment to justice action in society is undermined by the insistence that the United Church of Christ remain faithful to its modernist ways of thinking and working, faithful to an ecclesiology and polity that do not connect with a postmodern world. Means and ends are out of sync, to put it simply and bluntly.

Why Does All This Matter?

I have outlined the shift taking place in Western societies from modernity to postmodernity. And I have traced the evolution of United Church of Christ ecclesiology and polity as it became increasingly entangled with modernity. Why does all this matter? If the United Church of Christ does not confront this history and revise its ecclesiology and polity, the UCC will just as increasingly become estranged from the postmodern world and will increasingly flounder in its mission to seek justice, reconciliation, and liberation. Even if we could enlist more people, money, staff, and prophetic programming the results would still be the same, an increasingly sidelined religious institution in a postmodern world. This is a harsh judgment to which I have come with great reluctance. I wish it were not so; but I believe it is. I also believe that these are opportune times to review the history just described and to consider alternative ecclesiological and polity perspectives that will facilitate the mission of the United Church of Christ.

First, though, I need to show how this UCC history of entanglement with modernity impedes its mission. As the United Church of Christ has addressed the world with its prophetic call for justice for the poor and the oppressed, it has used typically modernist means of study papers, pronouncements, and resolutions passed by church bodies. These documents are intended to persuade policy makers, legislators, and administrators to become aware of injustice and to take remedial action. These same documents are also aimed at church members in the hope that they will join in speaking out to policy makers and legislators. Local churches are urged to study and support these positions. In spite of all this effort, the justice witness of the United Church of Christ rarely attracts media attention and exercises only modest political effect, because real political influence is shaped by lobbyists representing wealth and conservative political viewpoints. So the modernist heritage of study, argument, and persuasion relegates the United Church of Christ to the political margins of American society. Perhaps that is inevitable. How many UCC voters are there? How many UCC wealthy lobbyists and their interest groups can we muster? And is it even right to muster anyone, since our modernist belief is that each person needs to be persuaded but not manipulated or coerced?

United Church of Christ efforts to welcome and affirm diverse cultural and racial communities run up against these same modernist strictures. While the spirit of hospitality is genuine, the denomination dictates the terms of its hospitality through its ecclesiological and polity screens of modernity, requiring the adoption of UCC assumptions about autonomy, rationality, and due process. Thus we are baffled when the newcomers at the welcome table do not grasp the rules, or if they grasp them, do not like them, leading them to suggest other ways to be the church. We are particularly confused when such groups seem to interpret the Bible literally, or when they raise up charismatic pastors blessed by the Spirit rather than formally educated in a college and seminary, or when they insist on their own music filled with novel beats and imagery. At first all this diversity may enliven us in the midst of our constrained North European cultural practices, but then what? Are we truly ready to negotiate as equals a new kind of church life blending diverse cultural elements? Or will we insist, covertly if not overtly, that to be fully welcomed newcomers will have to become modernists as well as UCC church people?

The outreach of the United Church of Christ to youth and young adults, along with that of other mainline denominations, is similarly compromised in the postmodern world by our modernist procedural and ideological fixations. These newly minted postmodernists, with their technological savvy and visually imaginative ways of engaging their world, are not attracted to institutions or willing to commit their energies to institutions where participation in a supposedly rational process of decision-making is required. Postmoderns are aware, however, of power dynamics, and they understand that reasoned discussion and argumentation privilege the highly educated and verbally sophisticated, and at the same time drain the passion required for the energetic life of religious commitment. Not only are postmoderns uninterested in institutional governance via committees and boards; they are drawn to religious activities employing the musical and visual art forms that engage heart and soul, not those that primarily engage the mind. This is not to say that postmoderns are unreflective, but that such reflections are likely to depend on primary experiences that are more holistic. Life is not a problem to be solved rationally; life is to be lived intensely.

Our modernist UCC ecclesiology and polity compromise faithful mission not only as the church reaches out but also as the church looks within to fulfill its communal calling. Centered in Word and Sacrament, formed by its liturgical, educational, prophetic, and serving ministries, the church has a rich inner life that is fully engaged with its missional outreach, indeed without which mission would languish and vanish altogether. But our ecclesiological and polity statements suggest otherwise. They suggest a diminished or second-order role for the inner life of the church. In the draft *Manual on Church*, the phrase "beloved community" appears as one of the marks of the church. But the document intends this phrase to mean the community that is seeking justice and engaged in God's mission. One would think that "beloved community" might also embrace worship, community life (including potlucks!), educational experiences for all ages, a sense of caring and support during times of suffering, loss, and death, or attention to the stewardship of resources for the sake of mission. In the same document, a telling phrase appears: "Lest our community become too focused on itself,..." (lines 176–77). This warning about self-focus unfairly pits mission against a rich inner church life. Mission-oriented churches are that way because of their rich life of worship, preaching, study, sacramental life, and fellowship, not in spite of all that. Likewise the many declarations that the church exists for mission and not for itself, that institutional structures are not for themselves but for mission, along with all the references to the Mission of God in documents, speeches, and other writings, reinforce the impression that the inner life of the church is valuable only when it results in missional action.

The tone of this rhetoric about the church existing for mission suggests a low view of the church as community and institution. But the same missional rhetoric reflects a high view of movements for social transformation toward greater justice and calls the church to be such a movement. This call reflects both a modernist belief in progress and belief in the moral obligation to work for progress. It is a secular eschatology, a perfected future brought about by strenuous human effort, not by divine intervention or divine completion in which human responses are engaged but are not the sole agents of change. Such secular eschatologies lodged in modernist visions of a perfected society appeal to liberal and progressive churches like the United Church of Christ. They appear to be nearly equivalent to the promised peaceable kingdom depicted in scripture, and in Christian eschatological hope, and therefore worthy of church support. But a theologically faithful hope in God's future should result in greater critical discernment in the church, which in turn should help the church distance itself from its entanglement with modernist and progressive political agendas. This disentanglement should also encourage a greater appreciation for the inner life of the church and for its institutional character. Surely a greater commitment to the mission of the church would follow in its train.

Conclusion

In this chapter I have argued that a deliberate disentanglement from modernity is required if the United Church of Christ, and other mainline denominations, are to minister faithfully in the emerging postmodern world. I have also argued that we need to understand the transition from modernity to postmodernity, and to reexamine our own denominational history to understand how its ecclesiology and polity became entangled with modernity. This entanglement has grown into an unexamined orthodoxy of church practice to which we cling in spite of the ways it impedes faithful mission. Such a reexamination will be difficult and painful. But I believe it is urgent that we begin.

In the two concluding chapters, I propose alternative ecclesiological and polity perspectives for the United Church of Christ. I hope these proposals will foster the kind of exploration that might lead to theological and practical modifications that will facilitate the mission of the church. These are neither blueprints nor manifestos, simply proposals. By saying that I do not mean to take anything away from the urgency I feel about this challenge.

CHAPTER THREE

A Re-Visioned Ecclesiology
for Postmodern Times

I F THE UNITED CHURCH OF CHRIST is to survive in post-modernity, it will need to re-vision its ecclesiological identity. That will require a denomination-wide exploration and consensus-building addressing the nature and mission of the church of Jesus Christ. Whether that is possible and how it might happen are the questions discussed in this chapter.

It is difficult to imagine how the UCC, or other mainlines, for that matter, could engage in such a deliberate church-defining process. Not wanting to be taken for evangelicals or fundamentalists, mainline churches like the United Church of Christ tolerate and even encourage diverse theological beliefs, including beliefs about the church. In keeping with modernity, every church participant decides what to believe about traditional religious questions — God, Jesus, Spirit, human nature, the good life, and what happens after death. People participate in churches where they feel comfortable about how such questions are treated, where they are welcomed and feel at home, where positive attitudes prevail over human quirks and contentions, and where everyone seems to share common core values so that one can relax and not always be on guard, a persistent fear permeating daily life in the wider world.

Especially in a denomination like the UCC, where the only official or authoritative teaching offices are the individual conscience and the various expressions of the church — local churches, associations and conferences, the General Synod and its related bodies, speaking and acting only for themselves, never speaking for others or the whole church — it is difficult to imagine how a deliberate faith-based consensus about the church could be achieved. In spite of those cautions, I believe we must try to engage the whole United Church of Christ in rethinking the theological meaning of the church, which is the essence of ecclesiology. That will require church leaders who believe that defining ecclesiology is of paramount urgency, more urgent even than other concerns claiming their attention.

Ecclesiological urgency finally means recovering the identity of the church in a postmodern age. In the heyday of modernity the culture knew the nature and purpose of the church — to provide meaning and hope, and thus contribute to a stable social order. Though no longer arbiters of truth and morals as in the Middle Ages, churches were still thought to benefit modern society. Government-supported churches in European nations provided spiritual support for cultural and political unity. Even in the United States with its nonestablishment clause in the Bill of Rights, churches were still publicly valued as civilizing influences. This belief in the public values of churches shows up in the practice of property tax exemptions for land and buildings owned by religious organizations and used for religious purposes. During the heyday of modernity in the United States, particular denominations functioned as quasi-established religions — Congregationalists in New England, Presbyterians in the Middle Atlantic and Mid-South region, Methodists and Baptists in the Midwest and South, Episcopalians in Eastern urban centers, and Lutherans in the Upper Midwest. These denominations exerted a powerful public presence and voice. No one was compelled to join or financially support them, to be sure. But their identities were clear.

In the transition from modernity to postmodernity, these culturally settled church identities are fading away, and in some places have virtually disappeared altogether. Megachurches, seeker churches, emergent churches, and nondenominational churches have blurred or confused traditional denominational identities. Politically conservative movements like the Christian Coalition have used the Christian name as though it obviously requires Christians to oppose abortion, feminism, homosexuality, and environmentalism, the teaching of evolution, multiculturalism, and genetic manipulation. Claiming the Christian name for social conservatism makes moderate or liberal Christians hesitant about calling themselves Christians at all. Worse than that, militantly violent groups in Christianity, as well as in other religious traditions, justify physical assault and murder as acceptable means of extending the power of true religion.

In such a highly charged social environment, the United Church of Christ and other mainline denominations can assume nothing as given about the nature of the church and its place in postmodern culture, but must vigorously reclaim and restate their identities. Some denominational traditions can do this by reclaiming their normative confessional or liturgical traditions. The United Church of Christ, with a rich confessional heritage but no authoritative confessional standard, requires a renewed ecclesiology and polity to set forth its identity in a postmodern world. The UCC still-speaking God identity campaign emphasizes continuing divine revelation and core affirmations about peace with justice, being open and affirming, multicultural and multiracial, anti-racist, and accessible to all, as well as the call to practice radical hospitality, early truth telling, and evangelical courage. These efforts to position the UCC in its own self-awareness and in public awareness are not sufficient, however, and are often mistakenly supposed to arise from a liberal political perspective, or worse, to be simply political correctness in a religious guise. Only theological clarity about the nature and mission of the church can rectify these misperceptions, showing how UCC core commitments are solidly grounded in that mission. Ecclesiological clarity will not resolve conflicts over differing moral judgments among Christian bodies, or even within the UCC, but clarity can engage the disputants in addressing differences of theological interpretation rather than reducing them to conflicting political ideologies.

Where to begin with such an ecclesiological retrieval? Earlier I identified ecclesiological themes currently appearing in UCC discourse — the founding ecclesiology, a church of covenantal relations, a church engaged in the mission of God, the church as a beloved community, and the church as listening to the still-speaking God. These themes, not inherently contradictory but expressing differing accents, do not constitute, even if taken altogether, an adequate ecclesiology for postmodern times. That is because their theological assumptions are hidden or taken for granted. In modernity that strategy might have sufficed, since everyone knew what a church is and what it stands for. In postmodernity such clarity has been replaced by wildly diverse and extreme opinions about the church, fueled by personal or political animosity or by equally unrealistic claims that one's own church holds forth the only valid truth about God.

My proposals for reformulating United Church of Christ ecclesiology require, first of all, exploring the ecclesiological foundations of the United Church of Christ located in the two documents carrying the formal authority of votes taken by Congregational-Christian local churches and the synods of the Evangelical and Reformed Church — the Basis of Union of 1948, and the Constitution of 1961, particularly Paragraph 2 in the Preamble. In addition to these two voted documents, other weighty documents voted by General Synod and commended to the churches grounded in this founding ecclesiology — the Statement of Faith, the Book of Worship, the New Century Hymnal, and the Mission Statement — also need to be reviewed for their distinctive ecclesiological contributions. But behind all these sources are the ancient and Reformation affirmations about the church found in the Preamble, Paragraph 2, where Jesus Christ is acknowledge as "its [the UCC's] sole Head, Son of God and Savior"; where "the Word of God in the Scriptures" and the "presence and power of the Holy Spirit" constitute the church; where the "faith of the historic church" is claimed as set forth in "the ancient creeds and reclaimed in the basic insights of the Protestant Reformers"; where every generation must "make this faith its own in reality of worship, in honesty of thought and expression, and in purity of heart before God"; and where two sacraments are recognized — "Baptism and the Lord's Supper or

Holy Communion." These affirmations cite historic sources we need to consult again as we develop a revised ecclesiology for postmodern times.

The Ancient Creeds

Belief in the church became an article of faith in the Apostles' Creed ("the holy catholic church") and in the Nicene Creed (also known as the Nicene-Constantinopolitan Creed) of 381 ("one holy catholic and apostolic church"). These ancient marks of the church — unity, catholicity, holiness, and apostolicity — in addition to expressing a growing faith consensus of those times also reflected the need to guard the unity of the church against division.

For my purposes in proposing a revised United Church of Christ ecclesiology, I want to focus on the church as faithful to apostolic teaching as the ancient mark of the church that is most immediately fruitful in a postmodern age. The other marks are important and to be interpreted spiritually in postmodernity rather than institutionally, since institutional unification easily becomes an exercise of coercive power in which some rule over others in ways that debase the humanity of both.

Apostolicity as a mark of the true church means fidelity to the teaching of the apostles. In its earliest days as the Christian movement expanded in both Jewish and Roman circles, the first disciples of Jesus were accorded special honor because they knew Jesus in his earthly ministry. Though not a member of that group, Paul claimed equal apostolic status because of his encounter with the risen Christ on the road to Damascus. The writings thought to be authored by one of the apostles, or those closest to them like Luke and Mark, deserved preeminence as the church determined which writings had authority. The writings of the apostles, church leaders believed, would keep the church faithful to the teachings of Jesus and his ministry. While biblical scholars have long questioned the authenticity of traditional authorial attributions in the New Testament — James, Hebrews, some of Paul's letters, for example — the intent of the ancient compilers of scripture is clear: stay as close to Jesus as possible.

In the Middle Ages judging apostolic fidelity became the responsibility of bishops, for a time councils, but ultimately centered in the office of the pope. Protestant Reformers reclaimed the Bible as the sole authority for judging apostolic fidelity, with interpretive responsibility assigned variously to individual believers, pastors and teachers, or creeds and confessions. Reconciling conflicting scriptural interpretations became the endemic trouble spot for Protestants, though Catholics have also faced similar difficulties in fact, if not in official policy. Though in postmodernity it is agreed that ancient holy texts are not self-interpreting, it is equally clear that these texts cannot be made to say anything anyone wants them to say. It is up to each follower of Jesus Christ, and to each community of followers, to engage in scriptural interpretation prayerfully, invoking the guidance of the Holy Spirit.

The Basic Insights of the Protestant Reformation

This phrase from the Preamble invokes the Reformation agreements that the true church is found where the word is rightly preached and the sacraments rightly observed, to use Luther's phrase. Lutheran, Reformed, and Free Church traditions agreed on this principle, as did the Puritan Reformers in the Church of England. Calvin used several images for the church, speaking of it as "our mother," or speaking of the true church as all of the elect, while acknowledging that every actual church was composed of both the elect and the reprobate. Centering the church in word and sacrament was not a new thought, but by identifying the true church as those communities of valid word and sacrament, the Protestant Reformers rejected identifying the true church as communities ruled by bishops who, in turn, were under the rule of the Roman pontiff.

Protestant Reformation beliefs about the church are also found in the Preamble's opening affirmation: "The United Church of Christ acknowledges as its sole Head, Jesus Christ, Son of God and Savior," as well as in the declaration that: "It [the UCC] looks to the Word of God in the Scriptures, and to the presence and power of the Holy Spirit, to prosper its creative and redemptive work in the world." While churches of every kind would affirm that Jesus Christ is the sole head of the Church they would disagree about how Jesus Christ actually rules in the church. As I explained in the previous chapter, affirming Jesus Christ as the sole head of the church is both a critical and constructive principle. Critically this means that no office or assembly, secular or ecclesiastical, can act as head of the church. Constructively the sole headship of Jesus Christ means that Christ rules in the preaching of the word and celebration of the sacraments under the leading of the Holy Spirit. In the English Puritan tradition, particularly among the Independents, ministers of churches in their preaching and teaching exerted enormous influence in the spiritual and moral lives of their members, even though they possessed no official authority above that of the congregation. As this Independent and Puritan practice passed into modernity in the eighteenth and nineteenth centuries, Christ's rule in the local church was increasingly understood as the common mind of the congregation, arrived at by discussion and then settled by a vote of the members. While the mind of Christ was invoked in this decision-making process, it was often as much the political philosophy of voluntarism that came to occupy that uncertain place where the mind of Christ no longer seemed so clear. That is, the local church understood itself as composed of individuals voluntarily choosing to join it, where the collective will of the whole community needed the consent of the members.

Also reflecting a distinctly Protestant Reformation perspective is the declaration from the Preamble that "It [the UCC] looks to the Word of God in the Scriptures, and to the presence and power of the Holy Spirit to prosper its creative and redemptive work in the world." This invocation of Word and Spirit is meant to elevate their authority above other sources of divine revelation such as tradition, reason, or experience, to cite the example of the Wesleyan Quadrilateral. To elevate the authority of scripture and Spirit over other sources of revelation is faithful to the

Reformed tradition, but this principle does not always help discriminate among other sources of revelation. Setting aside the linguistic and conceptual difficulties with words like "reason" and "experience," I want here to disavow any Reformation denigration of tradition and to argue for its inclusion in the idea of the scriptural word. Tradition is not always a humanly devised catalog of beliefs set up in spite of or against scripture, as the Reformers sometimes thought. Rather tradition represents the effort of the church in each generation to work out practices and beliefs it judges to express scriptural teachings. Critical discernment, of course, must always be brought to the transmission and interpretation of the tradition, as it must also to the interpretation of biblical texts. Part of the constitutive character of the church, then, is not only its dependence on the scriptural Word in the power of the Spirit, but also in its critical appropriation of its traditions, without which the rich resources of centuries of Christian experience would be lost. The United Church of Christ, in its pronouncements, resolutions, and other deliberations draws on scriptural texts to support its causes, but seldom explicitly cites its traditions, or tucks them away in other parts of its declarations as though they were obviously and clearly in harmony with scripture.

Jesus Christ as Son of God and Savior

This phrase appears in the Preamble and in Article X of the Constitution on the definition of local churches. The verbs used are "acknowledging" [Preamble] and "believing" and "accepting" [Article X]. "Believe" and "bear witness" are the parallel verbs in the Basis of Union [Section II: Faith]. Another verb, "professing," is used in Article XI of the Constitution to describe how persons become members of a local church, by profession of faith, or by the profession of faith in Jesus Christ as Lord and Savior. The fact that the verb "confess" is not used in these foundational statements, or that the noun form, "confession," does not appear either, suggests that the founders believed that the United Church of Christ cannot have a confession of faith that is authoritative as in other denominations. While the United Church of Christ has a Statement of Faith that the General Synod commended for use in the churches, it is not a test of faith, only a testimony to a shared faith. None of these verbs suggests any weakening of a faithful response to Jesus Christ's invitation to follow him, but they do suggest a commitment to a growing relationship with Jesus Christ rather than agreement with propositional definitions.

Is anything essential lost in this nuanced language of believing, accepting, acknowledging, and professing? Not so long as their object remains Jesus Christ. So long as the United Church of Christ understands its relationship to Jesus Christ as foundational to the church and to the life of faith, a varied and nuanced list of verbs seems exactly what is needed in order to emphasize the relational character of faith and to avoid a definitional distortion of faith.

But when it comes to the name (Jesus) or titles (Christ, Savior, Lord, or God) used for that one in whom the church sees God fully present and humanity fully restored, then the traditional words are required, because any alternative takes something essential away. The name of Jesus, identifying the itinerant teacher and healer whose biography is briefly sketched in the canonical gospels, must continue to identify the one in whom the miracle and mystery of God's incarnation occurred. Though every person bears the divine image, using the name of Jesus of Nazareth is the only way to identify the particular person in whom God became fully incarnate.

The titles Jesus bears — Christ (messiah, anointed one), Son of God (divine intimacy), Lord (authority of God) and Savior (reconciling the cosmos and human history from futility to fulfillment in God) — these are all titles that set forth the fullness of divinity in Jesus Christ. These titles make it possible to know something of who God is and what God is doing in Jesus Christ. The United Church of Christ continues to use these titles from biblical, traditional, and ecumenical sources because they express, as much as human language will allow, the nature and function of the Jesus in whom God is fully present and at work. Many other words and images have been employed for the same purpose, and can be helpful. But these are the necessary titles, the ones we cannot do without — Christ, Son of God, Lord, and Savior.

What Is the Church to Do?

Called in grace to look to Jesus Christ as the sole head of the church, called to say that Jesus of Nazareth is the Christ, the Lord, Son of God and Savior — the church is called not only to receive that grace and make that profession with continual gratitude and joy, but also is called to share in Christ's mission in the world, for the sake of the whole world, not just for its own sake. The church becomes, quite literally as well as metaphorically, the body of Christ in the world.

In the Preamble the mission of the church is summarized in that very compact phrase, " . . . its [the United Church of Christ's] creative and redemptive work in the world." Then the Preamble speaks of " . . . the responsibility of the Church in each generation to make this faith its own in reality of worship, honesty of thought and expression, and in purity of heart before God." The scattered life of the church (creative and redemptive work in the world) and the gathered life of the church (worship, thought and expression, and purity of heart) are expressed together in the Preamble.

The same unity with dispersion in mission appears in Paragraph 10 of the Constitution where a local church is described as being " . . . organized for Christian worship, for the furtherance of Christian fellowship, and for the ongoing work of Christian witness." Here the balance seems to tilt toward the gathered life of the church, though "witness" can carry the full freight of mission in the world. While the Preamble speaks of recognizing " . . . two sacraments: Baptism and the Lord's Supper, or Holy Communion," and Paragraph 10 speaks of the church organizing "for Christian worship," with no mention of the sacraments, worship might still be understood to include them. But the sacramental centering of the church is not as evident as it should be in the Constitution.

This neglect is remedied in the Statement of Faith, where affirmations about the nature and mission of the church declare: "You bestow upon us your Holy Spirit, creating and renewing the church of Jesus Christ, binding in covenant faithful people of all ages, tongues, and races. You call us into your church to accept the cost and joy of discipleship, to be your servant in the service of others, to proclaim the gospel to all the world and resist the powers of evil, to share in Christ's baptism and eat at this table, to join him in his passion and victory." To begin with covenant, then discipleship, then service, then witness, then resistance, and finally sacramental fellowship creates an implied order of importance dear to the hearts of all in the UCC who emphasize the worldly mission of the church.

In answering the question of what the church is to do, once it is constituted by grace and a profession of faith, the Statement of Mission of the UCC, adopted by the General Synod in 1987, states the following: "To proclaim the Gospel of Jesus Christ in our suffering world; to embody God's love for all people; to hear and give voice to creation's cry for justice and peace; to name and confront the power of evil within and among us; to repent our silence and complicity with the powers of chaos and death; to preach and teach with the power of the living word; to join oppressed and troubled people in the struggle for liberation; to work for justice, healing and the wholeness of life; to embrace the unity of Christ's church; to discern and celebrate the present and coming reign of God." These phrases emphasize the mission of the church in the world, with less attention to the gathered life of the church. Concentrating on justice, peace, confronting evil and violence, working for liberation and healing, the Statement of Mission pays insufficient attention to an understanding of mission that includes the gathered life of the church — sacramentally gathered at font and table, before the pulpit where the word is preached, or in the educational, fellowship, and pastoral care dimensions of gathered church life. In the paper on ecclesiology for the Committee on Structures as it labored over the restructuring of 1999, there was an effort to redress this imbalance by identifying four persisting ecclesiological themes: "to proclaim the gospel in all the world; to gather and support communities of faith in their celebration and mission; to labor for the creation and increase of God's realm of justice and love in the world; [and] to manifest more fully the unity of the church, all humankind, and the whole creation."

The Committee on Structures also created, as part of its work on restructure, a background paper, "A Mission Framework for the General Synod Committee on Structure." The basic conviction set forth in this document states: "An ecclesiology which emerges from this conviction [*Missio Dei,* or mission of God] describes the church as essentially missionary. First the mission; then the church as the instrument of mission." One of the implications of this principle, according to this document, is that the church is defined as "... created by God for mission [and] lives its vocation only when it is engaged in mission." Later the same document states, "It is no longer theologically appropriate to continue a dichotomy between ecclesiological and mission structure. All ecclesiological entities exist because of mission...." Since this document does not explain the dichotomy between ecclesiology and mission that it detects, or the dichotomy that needs to be rejected, it is difficult to tell how framing ecclesial structure under the rubric of mission will fix anything. And though there are passing references to the gathered church in this document, it is clear that the church gathers only to empower the mission, not for other worthy purposes. While this document captures the ethos of the current national setting of the United Church of Christ focused on mission in the world on behalf of justice and peace, it unfortunately fails to express adequately the church's grounding in God's grace through Jesus Christ, who calls those who follow him to be the church engaged in a mission that embraces sacrament, word, fellowship, education, and mutual care, as well as mission in the world.

A Re-visioned Ecclesiology
for a Postmodern World

In light of the ecclesiological affirmations just surveyed from United Church of Christ sources and mindful of the challenges of postmodernity, I propose a re-visioned United Church of Christ ecclesiology summarized in the four following points:

1. *The church consists of all those who have answered the call of Jesus Christ to follow him.* To follow Jesus Christ is to receive the divine gifts of justification (meaning made righteous before God) and sanctification (meaning divinely aided to grow in the holiness of life and purity of heart that characterize life in Christ). To follow Jesus Christ is to live a life in keeping with Christ's teachings and example. To follow Jesus Christ is to join him in his passage from incarnate life through death to resurrection and heavenly reign, always with the promise of his return and the completion of his reign of justice and love. To follow Jesus Christ is to receive the gift of community, community with the triune God, and with all those who have answered Christ's call to follow him. In receiving the gift of the community with Christ and all who follow him, the Holy Spirit is present in and with that gift, providing inspiration, insight, and empowerment for mission. This reality of divinely given community with all who follow Jesus Christ means actual communities of followers, called churches, gathered in celebration and scattered in mission in the world. The church, therefore, is not just a useful adjunct to Christian life. It is an integral part of that life. Without participating in an actual church, Christian life is reduced to private belief or to solitary prayer or to unaided efforts to lead a good life. An imagined better church or true church not bound to actual churches may be a useful construct to increase awareness of ways the actual church falls short; but such a construct is not a substitute for life in an actual church.

Why do I prefer the verb "to follow" for explaining how the church of Jesus Christ is constituted? Why not use confess, or profess, or acknowledge, or affirm, or all those other verbs appearing in United Church of Christ foundational documents?

Those other verbs unduly lend themselves to constructing propositional statements of truth with which one must agree. While the church has always labored to find the proper words and construct the right sentences to express its understanding of the biblical faith, these statements have been used as a test of faith, determining who was a true believer and who was not. The United Church of Christ understands that all its confessions and covenants are testimonies to its shared faith, neither tests of proper belief, nor boundaries defining who is outside the circle of faith.

Using the phrase "to follow Jesus" means trusting him and remaining loyal to him. Following is a more relational verb than "confessing," "professing," or all the others. Followers of Jesus are, of course, called to express their faith in statements of belief, indicating what they believe and why they say it that way. But such statements are always living, breathing, and provisional documents, subject to the realization that God, indeed, is still speaking to the church, calling the church to act and believe in new ways. And following Jesus Christ as the action constituting the church allows for no presumptuous definitions of the true believer or the true church. All are called. Some have answered the call. Some have rejected the call. Some have paid no attention. The eternal standing of all these varied responses is not something for us to judge; it must be left to the gracious mercy and mystery of a loving God.

Why not use "discipleship" or "friendship" instead of the word "following"? "Disciple" is a scriptural word, used by the gospel writers for those Jesus called, and in John's gospel (14:14–15) Jesus calls his disciples friends, no longer servants, because they now understand who he is and what is coming. But "discipleship" and "friendship" have limitations not found in the more open and inclusive word "follower." Discipleship emphasizes the teaching–learning aspect of Jesus' relationship with his followers. That is a critically important dimension, but it does not fully capture everything embedded in the word "following" — the trust, the loyalty, the risk-taking, and the active role of the follower rather than the more passive role of the learner. Friendship is a rich metaphor of the embracing relationship we have to the God we know in Jesus Christ, full of the love, compassion, honesty, and challenges that characterize true human friendship. But using the word "friend" as the church-constituting term for those who follow Jesus Christ, might suggest the full mutuality and equality that characterize human friendships. We humans direct our laments and pleadings to God, to be sure, as well as our praise and love. But we never assume that we are friends with God or with Jesus Christ. We never assume that friendly equality with God is our human aim or is included in the divine gift. The distance between ourselves and God is still too fraught with mystery, awe, wonder, and sometimes fear. It is a relationship of sharp inequality as well as a relationship of companionate love. Such a relationship cannot be subsumed under the heading of friendship.

2. *The church, constituted of those who have answered the call to follow Jesus Christ, gathers at the font, the pulpit, and the table where Jesus Christ is truly present as the sole head of the church, and where the Holy Spirit inspires and empowers the church for Christ's mission in the world.* Constituted by all those who have answered the call to follow Jesus Christ, the church is ordered in its gathered life by the font, the pulpit, and the table, where Christ's presence and rule are most visibly and powerfully experienced. This ordered life of the gathered church is expressed in its liturgical practices for corporate worship — weekly Sunday worship and special liturgical occasions — but also in its communal practices of educating adults and children in the Christian life and for mission, of occasions for intergenerational and group fellowship where mutual care and support are learned and practiced, of occasions for managing the organizational structures of the church along with care for its physical plant and properties, and occasions of engaging the wider ecumenical church and other religious communities. In all of these practices of the church, the font, pulpit, and table are the ordering sacraments of God's grace. These sacraments may be in the shadows, or in the deep background at a church

potluck or at a congregational meeting to debate the budget for the coming year. But the sacraments are always there, ordering the church. Constitutions, bylaws, and policy statements, as well as rules of procedure like Robert's, may unintentionally encourage churches to think of themselves as voluntary institutions where, as in a political democracy, the will of the people is sovereign. But it is not so in the church. The rule of Jesus Christ prevails. The voice of the people is clearly not the voice of God.

Christ's rule in a sacramentally ordered church is manifest, first of all, at the font, where the cleansing and refreshing waters of baptism signify both the death of the old self and the rebirth of the new person in Jesus Christ and the radical, unqualified welcome accorded the baptized by the church, where the first word is literally "welcome to new life in Christ," where the next word is "whoever you are now, you are loved unconditionally with a divine grace beyond human comprehension," and then where the third word is "welcome to Christ's ministry and mission in the world, where you will receive gifts for mission from the Holy Spirit, enabling you to witness and serve in ways you never imagined possible." Christ's rule at the font, then, is an act of welcoming, cleansing, of a new birth, and of receiving gifts for ministry. Wherever any actual church fails to manifest this baptismal aspect of Christ's reign, it has become a disordered church or, no church at all. When that happens, the baptismal reign of Christ must be brought to bear against that church on behalf of its repentance and renewal. Often that prophetic witness against a church that has lost its baptismal center must come from its regional or national church structures or their staff. In the United Church of Christ baptism is identified in the Preamble, the Basis of Union, and the Statement of Faith as one of the two sacraments in the Protestant traditions. While United Church of Christ rituals of baptism, as in the *Book of Worship*, are faithful to our historic and contemporary ecumenical agreements on baptism, it is unfortunate that baptism's infrequent observance diminishes an awareness of Christ's baptismal rule. A small font at the front of a church's worship space seldom is as visually prominent as the pulpit or table. A larger font with running water at the back of the church, with a personal discipline of pausing there for prayer and ritual sprinkling on entering, might facilitate a greater awareness of Christ's rule from the font. It would also help to employ liturgies of baptismal renewal more frequently, with water poured and sprinkled throughout the gathered congregation.

The pulpit is also a sacramental ordering of the gathered life of the church where Jesus Christ rules. It seems odd that the Protestant Reformers of the sixteenth and seventeenth centuries retained baptism and holy communion as the only approved sacraments while, at the same time, giving such prominence to preaching and hearing the word from the scriptures, but without thinking of preaching as sacramental. Whatever the reasons for the Reformers' sacramental hesitations, it was clear in Lutheran, Reformed, and in many of the Free Church traditions from the Protestant Reformation that Jesus Christ was truly present in the reading and preaching of the scriptural word. In contemporary United Church of Christ practice, this centrality of preaching persists even if sacramental theological reasons are remote or missing altogether. The fact that good preaching is always a prominent measure of a candidate's appeal as judged by congregational search committees shows how important the sermon is. In addition to the belief that Jesus Christ is present in the preached word and therefore exercises his church headship through this medium, preaching is also believed to be inspired by the Holy Spirit. Prayers invoking the Spirit appear at the beginning of the liturgy of the word, not just in the Eucharistic liturgy. Word and Spirit joined in the preaching and hearing of the divine word comprise a second way or ordering the life of the church, the gathered community of those following Jesus Christ.

And, in the third place, the church gathered at the table where the broken bread and the poured wine are shared shows itself to be ordered by Jesus Christ who is its sole head. Christ is himself present, not just in the elements, but also in the liturgical action of the whole community of his followers gathered at the table. There Jesus Christ is remembered; there Jesus Christ instructs his followers afresh and renews their faltering breathing with the very breath of the Holy Spirit as in that Easter upper room described in John's gospel; there, at the table, Christ's followers are refashioned as his own sacramental presence for the sake of the world, as Christ's living body broken and then raised to new life for the sake of the world; and there the followers of Jesus Christ share a foretaste of that heavenly banquet where all will rejoice in the fullness of divine hospitality. In the liturgy of the table communal prayers of petition and intercession, of confession, and of thanksgiving give form to the divine–human encounter at the heart of table fellowship. There at the table the inner life of devotion and the outer life of prophetic witness for justice are nurtured and empowered.

3. *Constituted by those who follow Jesus Christ, ordered in its gathered life by the sacraments of font, word, and table, the church is also perpetually scattered in the world engaged in Christ's mission of compassionate love, prophetic witness to God's justice, and action on behalf of that justice.* This third ecclesiological principle requires the disciplined engagement of Christ's followers in social analysis to discern where compassionate love and justice are most needed, and in effective personal and collective witness and action on their behalf. Discerning the need for compassionate justice needs is sometimes easy and obvious — where oppression and violence diminish or destroy the humanity of marginalized social classes; poor people; religious, racial, and ethnic groups; or on the basis of gender, sexual orientation, or handicapping conditions. Even there it is often hard to know how to witness and act effectively. In other situations God's justice is not so evident. Decisions about the beginning and ending of human life; decisions about morally appropriate uses of genetic technology; or apportioning scarce health care or educational resources, for example, must engage the church, but without being quite as sure of the divine mandate. God's justice mandate would seem obviously on the side of protecting the environment, but to what degree and with what means? And if the church is to "resist the powers of evil," as the Statement of Faith declares, what means of resistance can be morally justified

by a church committed to a just peace, or peace with justice? Is passive resistance the only acceptable way, or is armed resistance ever appropriate, even with its deadly consequences? Engaging such questions of moral judgment and appropriate action are a necessary part of the ministry of Christ's followers in the world. These issues range from the obvious and simple all the way to the complex and difficult. Following Jesus Christ means immersion in them, as ways of loving the neighbor that are just as important as a friendly visit or a loving embrace.

4. *The ministry of oversight in the United Church of Christ is exercised by local communities of ministry in covenant with associations (or conferences acting as associations), and with conference ministers.* Local communities of ministry oversee their ministries under the sole lordship of Jesus Christ, but for the sake of their well-being are in turn overseen by associations and conference ministers, who are also under the lordship of Jesus Christ. This pastoral oversight, always in mutually covenanted relationships, is concerned with the calling of authorized ministers to lead communities of ministry and with the standing of authorized ministries and local communities of ministry within the larger ecclesial family. While the Constitution of the United Church of Christ is clear about the freedom and autonomy of local churches (Paragraph 18) and about the authority of associations in the standing of ministers and local churches (Paragraphs 40 and 41), in practice these relationships are understood as purely voluntary, especially on the part of local churches. The *Manual on Ministry* has always characterized itself as a description of practices commonly shared in the UCC, not as a body of laws or regulations. Fanning flames of fear about top-down authoritarianism has been a favorite ploy of those who acknowledge accountability only to themselves or their local churches. But in fact the Constitutional foundations for mandating shared oversight already exist, though they are rarely invoked against the absolute language used in Paragraph 18. To say, therefore, that oversight in the United Church of Christ is exercised in mutually covenanted relationships is not to say they are purely voluntary. They are given and mandated

not just in the Constitution, but by the same Jesus Christ who, in calling the church into being, brings forth gifts of oversight for the well-being of the whole church. It is therefore not a matter of Constitutional revision, but only of changes in the culture and practices of the UCC that a faithful ministry of oversight by associations requires.

The conference minister, however, is not currently a minister of oversight provided in the Constitution. The Bylaws state that "a conference employs such salaried personnel as its program may require" (Paragraph 168), surely a weak and vague permission for program staffing without any necessarily pastoral oversight. In practice, however, the uniting denominations exercised regional pastoral oversight through Conference Superintendents in the Congregational–Christian denomination and Synod Presidents in the Evangelical and Reformed Church. Modern ecumenical statements on the church — *Baptism, Eucharist, and Ministry*, the *Consultation on Church Union Consensus*, and *The Nature and Mission of the Church* — identify a growing ecumenical convergence on a threefold ministry, consisting of oversight (or bishop), local church pastor (or presbyter or elder), and deacon. Denominations in the Reformed and Free Church traditions, like the United Church of Christ, with their histories of corporate or local oversight rather than individual oversight, have not warmed to the idea of the bishop as a necessary office of pastoral oversight. But these Reformed denominations still, in the practice, have offices of oversight with other names — synod or presbytery executive, regional or area minister, conference minister, association minister, and the like. None of these offices carry the weighty official authority of bishops for maintaining fidelity to the apostolic faith or for the unity of the church, but they still perform many of the same pastoral functions. The United Church of Christ needs, in postmodernity, to identify its office of conference minister as having authority, along with association committees on ministry, for the well-being of churches and authorized ministers in their jurisdictions.

In concluding and summarizing this discussion of a re-visioned ecclesiology for the United Church of Christ, the four ecclesiological principles discussed above must be at the center of such a process — the church as constituted by those who follow Jesus Christ; the gathered community of the followers of Jesus Christ, the church, as it is ordered by Jesus Christ gathered at the font, by the word, and at the table; the scattered followers of Jesus Christ empowered by him as they engage the world in ministries of compassionate care and justice action; and the oversight of mission in ministries in covenant with associations and conference ministers.

One ecclesiological question remains: Having identified the office of conference minister as an office of oversight, what about other authorized ministers in the church — ordained, commissioned, and licensed ministers? Are such offices also constituent aspects of ecclesiology? In the United Church of Christ, as in other Reformation traditions, these authorized ministers are understood to be called by the Spirit and equipped with gifts of leadership skill and knowledge. Unlike the Catholic traditions where priests are ordained by bishops in the apostolic succession, Protestant traditions hold that the pastoral office is a gift from the Word in the power of the Holy Spirit in order that the church can fulfill its calling as Christ's body engaged in his mission in the world. Discerning these gifts and certifying them by the rite of ordination expresses the conviction that the call of God through Jesus Christ in the power of the Holy Spirit is at work in guiding the church and those called into the pastoral offices. These pastoral leaders are not called or appointed or elected, however much it may seem that way in practice. An important part of a re-visioned ecclesiology in the United Church of Christ will be a renewal of theological conviction about those called to lead the church. This renewal must not, of course, be at the expense of personal qualities, skills, or knowledge properly expected of church leaders. But the calling to ministry leadership in the church is finally more than a sum of professional expectations. The church finally discerns who is qualified by the gifts of the Spirit and the call of

Jesus Christ. Even though ecclesiologies in the Reformed and Free Church traditions have been reluctant to insist that only the ordained can preach, teach, preside, or pastorally lead the church, these churches have nevertheless practiced such restrictions, where possible, in the conviction that properly called and ordained leaders could better lead the liturgies and teach their meanings than someone temporarily called up from the community. Putting the matter more abstractly and theologically, in the Free Church and Reformed traditions at the heart of the United Church of Christ, the essential being of the church does not require an ordained office, but its well-being does.

Ecclesiologies Compared

I have just sketched four principles for re-visioning United Church of Christ ecclesiology:

the church constituted by those answering the call of Jesus Christ to follow him;

the gathered church ordered by Jesus Christ at the font, the pulpit, and the table;

the scattered church in the world engaged in Jesus Christ's mission of compassionate love and justice action;

and the pastoral oversight of associations and conference ministers.

These need now to be compared with ecclesiological themes currently present in UCC belief and practice. Earlier I identified these themes: (1) the church as covenant community practicing covenantal relations; (2) the church as beloved community; (3) the church as called to engage in the mission of God; and (4) the church as practicing radical hospitality attentive to the still-speaking God. These comparisons should show whether my proposals add anything substantively new and important to UCC ecclesiology.

The church as covenant community is a prominent theme in the book by Randi Jones Walker entitled *The Evolution of a*

UCC Style.[11] She also speaks of a three-part ecclesiology using the concepts of beloved community, covenantal life, and mission of God. I will comment on the idea of the church as beloved community shortly, but first I want to speak of covenantal relations or covenantal life because of its prominence in defining UCC polity. In the teaching and writings of Louis Gunnemann, but also in writings and speeches by Ruben Sheares and Avery Post, the emerging polity of the United Church of Christ was defined as a polity of covenant, in contrast to traditional episcopal, presbyterial, or congregational polities. Covenant meant, in the way they used the word, the obligation in the United Church of Christ for all its settings or expressions — local churches, associations, conferences, and the General Synod with its related national bodies, to engage one another with respect and honor, speaking to one another and listening to one another for the sake of the well-being of the whole church. This covenantal theme was based on examples of biblical covenants, as well as covenant theology in the Reformed and Puritan traditions. But as I said earlier, the idea of a covenantal polity, with its norms of respect and trust where authority is shared equally but always voluntarily, seems a far cry from the sterner stuff of Hebrew Bible or Puritan covenant theology, where God sets the terms of the covenant and enforces them when fallible humans break covenant promises. This confusion of terminology about UCC polity seems equally problematic if UCC ecclesiology claims that the church is fundamentally, or at least partially, a covenant community. In her chapter on "Congregationalism and Its Discontents," Randi Walker links traditional Congregationalist belief in local church autonomy with the notion of a covenant that binds autonomous churches together for the sake of the unity of the whole church, part of the professed aim of the United Church of Christ. But while Walker thoroughly describes the strands of covenant running through the historic traditions comprising the United Church of Christ, she does not sufficiently ground these covenant themes on UCC ecclesiology, on the call of God through Jesus Christ, or in the constituting of the church through decisions to follow him, and the sacramental ordering of the church in its inner life and its mission in the world. For Walker it is the language of God's covenant with the church, God's mission in the world, but that way of speaking does not sufficiently ground ecclesiology in Jesus Christ or take sufficient note of the empowerment of the Holy Spirit. Any attempt, then, like Walker's or others who speak about a covenantal polity and covenantal ecclesiology without explicit reference to Jesus Christ and the Holy Spirit, will not sufficiently explain in a postmodern world why covenant relations are crucial for the life of the church. To put it another way, a covenantal ecclesiology is insufficiently grounded within its own terminological framework to be clearly understood in postmodernity. Too much is assumed, or taken for granted, like a modernist theory of political organization governed by the consent of the members. To put it more bluntly, in the UCC we are not a democracy. We are communities of the followers of Jesus Christ.

The church as beloved community is also an ecclesiological theme appearing nowadays in United Church of Christ discourse. In the *Manual on Church,* a document currently circulated for study by the Parish Life and Leadership Team in the national Local Church Ministries covenanted ministry, the term "beloved community" is introduced with the following words: " . . . with Christ we form what many call the beloved community. . . . We see the idea of the church as beloved community in the United Church of Christ's engagement with the ideal of becoming a multi-cultural, multi-racial church, open and affirming of lesbian, gay, bi-sexual and trans-gendered persons, accessible to and inclusive of all people regardless of ability" (lines 160–67).

As noted earlier, Randi Walker's ecclesiological formula begins with beloved community. Walker speaks of the beloved community this way: "While covenant is the ecclesiological idea most often associated with congregationalism, what first makes a congregation of people a church is the hope of a beloved community, a place where a person loves and is loved, and thus experiences tangibly the presence of God."[12] Walker cites the ecclesiological writings of Lewis S. Mudge, Presbyterian theologian, who writes about the beloved community. Mudge says this: "The words [beloved community] suggest not a smug gathering of 'the good,' but the community of sinners whom God loves. 'Beloved Community' is the communal creation of the 'One who loves in freedom.' Potentially, it involves everyone."[13]

Mudge, in turn, draws on the concept of beloved community from the writings of Josiah Royce, American Idealist philosopher of the late nineteenth and early twentieth centuries. Royce emphasized the communal aspect of life, rather than individualism. In his philosophy of religion, Royce argued that the "religion of Jesus" and the "religion about Jesus" were held together in the reality of the community of Christ's followers. This was and remains a community of individuals to be sure, but their communal reality as followers loyal to Jesus Christ makes them a sign and foretaste of the beloved community intended for all. Royce sums up his thinking about the beloved community in these words:

> . . . since the office of religion is to aim towards the creation on earth of the Beloved Community, the future task of religion is the task of inventing and applying the arts which shall win men over to unity, and which shall overcome their original hatefulness by the gracious love, not of mere individuals, but of communities. . . . Judge every social device, every proposed reform, every national and every local enterprise by the one test: *Does this help towards the coming of the universal community?* [italics in original][14]

The concept of beloved community, as employed by Walker, Mudge, and Royce is rich in ecclesiological implications, but standing alone or coming first, the concept of beloved community fails to give an account of the ground of the love given and received in community. Families, school groups, athletic teams, recovery groups, or people who work closely together in varied social settings could all be examples of beloved communities. But there the love they share does not need to be attributed to God. Walker speaks, as noted above, of the beloved community as that place where a person "experiences tangibly the presence of God," but she does not further explain how this could be. Is God tangibly present in every communal experience of loving and being loved? Surely some kind of definition or image of love is required before answering that question. Beloved community is surely a consequential ecclesiological concept, but not a place where one can begin. One must begin with the experience of God's love in Jesus Christ calling people to follow him. That is the love constituting the church, which indeed becomes an expression of the beloved community, but not prior to its constitution in God's grace in Jesus Christ.

The church as the mission of God is a third ecclesiological theme appearing currently in the United Church of Christ. The mission of God, or in its Latin form, *Missio Dei*, is a conviction about the church stated by David J. Bosch in his book *Transforming Mission: Paradigm Shifts in Theology of Mission*. Bosch argues that "mission is not primarily an activity of the church but an attribute of God. God is a missionary of God. . . . Mission is thereby seen as a movement from God to the world; the church is viewed as an instrument of that mission. The church is there because there is mission, not vice versa."[15] In the document "A Mission Framework for the General Synod Committee on Structure," published for the twenty-first General Synod in 1997, it is argued that *Missio Dei* is the basic framework for the structure of any church, concluding that "it is no longer theologically appropriate to continue a dichotomy between ecclesiology and mission structure. All ecclesiological entities exist because of mission."[16] In the next paragraph, Bosch's description of mission is cited, using his words, as "mediating salvation, the quest for justice, evangelism, contextualization, liberation, enculturation, common witness, as done by the whole people of God."[17]

Arguing that the mission of God, or *Missio Dei,* comes before ecclesiology, or is the foundation of ecclesiology, is problematic on two grounds: Its implied view of God, illustrated in the sentence from Bosch quoted above, "God is a missionary of God," is nonsensical conceptually and absurd both theologically and philosophically. "Mission of God" as a term suggests there are two gods at work here, one sending and the other going out on mission in the world. To give Bosch the benefit of the doubt, one might attribute his rhetoric to the need to dramatize diverse functions of the persons of the Trinity, with God sending Jesus Christ on mission into the world in the power of the Spirit. But that does not seem to be the case. Theologically and philosophically the concept of *Missio Dei* fails to take account of the historic conviction that the God who created the universe and who providentially orders its life is the same loving and just God revealed in Jesus Christ, and that while God calls the church into being in Jesus Christ and calls it to a missional vocation, *Missio Dei* takes too much away from God's providence and gives too much responsibility to those who believe they know what God is trying to accomplish through their own missional labors. That shift in emphasis from divine providence to human responsibility turns the gospel into urgent action mandates rather than the good news of God's grace. Then come inevitably striving, a mix of success and failure, and finally guilt over having not done enough.

The value of the idea of the mission of God can be realized if it is reframed as the mission of the church, or as the mission of Jesus Christ in calling the church into being and sending it on mission in the world. That is precisely the claim made in my third ecclesiological principle proposed earlier. But when advocates for *Missio Dei* insist that mission comes first, before the church; insist that mission is the only reason for the existence of the church; and call it the mission of God rather than the mission of the church or Jesus Christ, I must disagree with the claim that *Missio Dei* could be a genuine ecclesiological option. It takes too much for granted, neglecting the foundation of the church in the call to follow Jesus Christ and the ordering of the church for its gathered life and mission in the world under the guidance of the Holy Spirit. *Missio Dei* also assumes that we know what God's mission actually is and that our reluctance to step out and just do it comes from lives privileged by the unjust way things are ordered, and from a lack of courage. Undoubtedly those are accusations justly made. But they are not the good news of the gospel. Only when we answer the call of Jesus Christ to follow him and experience Christ's transformation from death to life can we risk justice action joyfully, not grimly. Unfortunately the rhetoric of the mission of God, *Missio Dei,* appears widely these days in UCC sermons, speeches, and documents. In a significant way this phrase has come to express who we are and what we are about. Sadly this phrase cannot carry that load. Only the decision to follow Jesus Christ and experience his transformation from death to life can do that. We need to say so.

The church listening to the still-speaking God is a fourth ecclesiological theme prominent in the United Church of Christ. The UCC embarked on its public awareness campaign in 2003, called the "still-speaking initiative," as a way of demonstrating its identity with visual images, by means of TV commercials, posters and banners, clothing, mugs, bumper-stickers, pins, and other items. Its admonition, "Never place a period where God has placed a comma!" attributed to comedian Gracie Allen, has provided the core image of the campaign, a red comma on a black field. The TV commercials affirm that whoever you are and wherever you are on life's journey, you are welcome in the United Church of Christ. This campaign affirms two theological principles: (1) God is still speaking, meaning that the divine word is not confined to the words of scripture, nor must the word of God today be simply a repetition of something already said in the Bible; God continually offers a new word. And (2) the United Church of Christ is a church of extravagant welcome, embracing all who will enter, regardless of race, culture, sexual orientation, wealth or poverty, and handicapping conditions. This extravagant welcome comes to the church and through the church to the world from the God who is still speaking.

There are ecclesiological suggestions in these still-speaking affirmations, but there is no developed ecclesiology as such. To say that churches in the UCC welcome diversity is more a declaration of missional obligation than it is a verifiable proposition. One wonders how many church shoppers, on visiting a nearby UCC church after seeing one of the commercials, actually experienced the extravagant welcome promised, particularly if there was something about them that did not fit the culture of the visited congregation.

Though the UCC affirmation of diversity is well illustrated in its TV commercials, the particular diversity where a still-speaking God becomes a key interpretive principle concerns differing sexual orientations and practices. Here is an issue where the weight of historical Christian moral theology has not been open and affirming. Even if interpreters demonstrate how the few biblical texts apparently addressing homosexuality do not truly constitute a rejection of a same-sex orientation or practice, the whole question is opened up in a new way if the still-speaking God is saying something quite new, outside and against the church's predominant moral tradition on this subject, a new divine word that is affirming rather than judging. But how is such a new divine word discerned? One might cite the radical hospitality practiced and taught by Jesus, in which the outcasts of his day were welcomed to the banquet hall and given the best seats at the table. Or someone might report a spirit-inspired vision urging the church to open its doors and welcome the previously excluded. Or someone might bring to the discernment process the pain of exclusion and violence visited upon persons of LGBT orientations, along with the growing consensus among mental health professionals and scientists that homosexuality is neurologically and genetically based, and is clearly not a lifestyle one chooses. This would be a typical discernment scenario in the United Church of Christ, though perhaps with some modesty about claiming divine authority for such conclusions. Declaring that God is still speaking puts the burden of proof for new viewpoints that contradict traditional church teachings on a discernment process in which scripture and tradition are not simply set aside, but rather are explored for options hitherto hidden under the accretion of traditional teaching.

However that process goes, it seems clear that the ecclesiological implications of the still-speaking initiative lie in the direction of a Spirit-guided church, not rejecting the triune God for radical Pentecostalism, but surely placing heavier emphasis on the

Holy Spirit than has been the case in the Western theological heritage. Whether the UCC can move into a more spirit-directed or even Pentecostal way of being a church remains to be seen. The dominant Enlightenment tradition of a university-educated ministry and the large number of professionals and educators in the UCC might make it difficult to move in that direction, though with increasing cultural and racial diversity, a more spirit-filled church culture is not out of the question. Clearly, though, the still-speaking initiative does not offer a genuinely alternative ecclesiology. Instead, it offers a differing emphasis within traditional ecclesiological formulations based on the triune God. The church would still be constituted by answering the call of Jesus Christ to follow him and would still be ordered by the font, the pulpit, and the table. But the church would direct its attention in greater measure to the continuing work of the Holy Spirit as the Spirit inspires and directs the church.

Other United Church of Christ Identity Themes

The General Synod pronouncement of 1993 calling on the United Church of Christ to become a "multi-racial and multi-cultural church accessible to all" initiated the formation of a series of phrases that became an identity mantra in the UCC — a "just peace, open and affirming, multiracial and multicultural church accessible to all," as a way to state the UCC mission in the world as well as calling itself to account when it falls short. Later one phrase was amended, "peace with justice," and one added: "anti-racist." Along with these widely used phrases, another list describing the church needed for the twenty-first century was adopted by that same 1993 General Synod. The United Church of Christ was called to become a church "attentive to the word, inclusive of all people, responsive to God's call, and supportive of one another." John Thomas, General Minister and President, coined phrases characterizing the UCC that are now widely used — a church of "extravagant welcome, early truth-telling, and evangelical courage." I cite these popular phrases in order to ask whether, individually or taken together, they represent an alternative ecclesiology, or whether they are grounded in some less obvious ecclesiology than those already considered. I believe that these phrases do not represent a substantively different ecclesiology. The church makes these commitments by discerning how the followers of Jesus Christ are called to live together in the church and how they are called to love the world and to witness and act for justice. But the ecclesiology warranting these commitments often seems hidden from view, both within the church and by those outside the church. It is not always obvious or even clear why the United Church of Christ speaks or acts as it does. As the United Church of Christ moves into postmodernity, it needs to explain more vigorously and clearly how these commitments arise from the decision to follow Jesus Christ and to serve Christ faithfully in and through the gathered and scattered life of the church. Only then can any ideological or political odium attached to these commitments be definitively refuted.

My conclusion about all these ecclesiological themes and identity phrases in the United Church of Christ is essentially the same conclusion I reached in an article previously published on this subject,[18] namely, that while they may present differing accents, these ecclesiological themes and phrases do not represent competing ecclesiologies, only diverse expressions of a shared ecclesiology often hidden from view, most fully represented in the early founding documents of the UCC, the Basis of Union, the Preamble to the Constitution, and the Statement of Faith. Each ecclesiological theme adds something important to our shared understanding of how the church is called to bear faithful witness in each time and place. But there is no new ecclesiology in them.

Constitutional Implications of a Re-visioned Ecclesiology

If the United Church of Christ re-visions its ecclesiology in the direction I propose in this chapter, one term, "Local Church," which appears frequently in the Constitution and Bylaws will need to be changed throughout those documents. A new Paragraph 18 will need to be substituted for the current version. And then one new paragraph will need to be added to Article VIII, Associations and Conferences.

Redefining the Local Church

I propose, first, that wherever the words "Local Church" appear in the Constitution and Bylaws, the words "Local community of ministry and mission" be substituted. In the current Constitution Paragraph 9 states, "The basic unit of the life and organization of the United Church of Christ is the Local Church." This assertion mistakenly equates a sociological entity, the voluntary association we call a local church in American society, with an ecclesiological conviction about the communities of those who follow Jesus Christ. For most of us, Local Church suggests a familiar organizational pattern — a voluntary membership organization with a building or campus, a ministerial and program staff, Sunday worship and other special services, an educational program, mission outreach and programs for the community, a budget, and all the other familiar accoutrements. This confusion of ecclesiological and institutional language has produced, in UCC history, the settled conviction that local churches are normative and that all other communities of ministry must be dependently related to local churches. The Constitution and Bylaws along with the *Manual on Ministry* perpetuate this confusion by grounding everything ecclesial in the local church.

To be sure there are practical reasons for this confusion of terms. Local churches raise and distribute the mission funds to support other expressions of the church — associations, conferences, and the General Synod with its covenanted ministries, as well as specialized ministries, such as institutional chaplaincies, urban ministries, campus ministries, theological seminaries, outdoor ministries, and all the rest. Regional and national settings of the denomination depend on that support, and in turn provide programs and services to local churches. But that institutional dependence on local churches should not be confused with the ecclesiological principle that the followers of Jesus Christ are gathered into local communities of ministry and mission. There is also a historical/theological reason for this confusion of terminology. Independents and Separatists in the English Reformation, as noted earlier, believed that local churches possessed the necessary gifts of word, sacrament, and order, with nothing essential added by assemblies, synods, councils, bishops, or other offices. This doctrine was carried over into New England Congregationalism and further developed there. But to apply this sixteenth- and seventeenth-century ecclesiological principle to local churches in modern and postmodern American society has the effect of absolutizing the institution of the local church at the expense of other local institutional church forms.

To substitute the phrase, "local community of ministry and mission," for "local church," wherever that phrase appears in the Constitution and Bylaws, would affirm an ecclesiological parity for local churches; hospital, military, and other institutional chaplaincies; specialized ministries on college, university, and theological school campuses; urban and rural specialized ministries; house churches; and for other actual or envisioned institutional forms of a local community of ministry and mission. We would have to learn to think and act in new ways, for example, understanding that the sacrament of baptism and rituals of church membership belongs as much to these other church forms as to local churches. Local communities of ministry and mission that are not presently local churches would need to decide, for themselves, if they are indeed such communities and not just places where ordained clergy are employed dispensing sacramental ministries, pastoral care, and preaching the word. Local churches, as they are now called, would no longer be required to be symbolically, and usually marginally, present in order that a sacramental celebration somewhere other than in a local church could be judged valid.

It is difficult to imagine that such ingrained habits of thought about the local church could be changed by the new terminology

I am proposing, "local communities of ministry and mission." It is also difficult to imagine that those believing that only the local church can ecclesiologically be the basic unit of the church will be drawn to a discussion of the church that might broaden the definition of church. It is even a bit ironic that in a church that values diversity and hospitality, other forms of local communities of ministry and mission cannot presently be welcomed and accredited, since they are not local churches. In spite of all these difficulties, I do believe that a conversation about the church in the United Church of Christ is urgently needed, a conversation that will genuinely entertain options like those I have been discussing.

Redefining Autonomy

Second, I propose that Paragraph 18 of the UCC Constitution be rewritten. This is the paragraph that asserts that "the autonomy of the Local Church is inherent and modifiable only by its own actions." This paragraph is alarmist and suspicious in tone and substantively misleading. The tone is set by such phrases as, "Nothing...shall destroy or limit the right of each Local Church," or in the same sentence, nothing "shall be construed as giving to the General Synod, or to any Conference or Association, now, or at any future time, the power to abridge or impair the autonomy of any Local Church."

The affairs to be managed solely by the autonomous local church, in Paragraph 18, include such responsibilities as determining its own organizational structure, worship and education, charter and name, constitution and bylaws, covenants and confessions of faith, the admission and dismissal of members, the call and dismissal of pastors, the ownership of property and management of its financial affairs, and the right to withdraw from the denomination at any time without forfeiting its property. It is with this list of affairs solely under the control of the autonomous local church that Paragraph 18 becomes substantively misleading, indeed clearly contradictory when compared with Paragraphs 40 and 41, where the standing of Local

Churches and the standing of ordained ministers are clearly lodged in the association. The verbs used in 40 and 41 are simple declarative verbs — "is, determines, confers, and certifies" — in Paragraph 40 on the standing of local churches, or in 41, "grants, certifies, transfers, and terminates," ordained ministerial standing. And in Paragraph 22 on ordination, declarative verbs also appear — "recognizes and authorizes that member whom God has called to ordained ministry" — verbs used to speak of Associations, not Local Churches, which only "cooperate" in ordinations. There is nothing subjunctive about the mood of these verbs, no "might" or "could" appear, nothing to qualify the authority of associations in the standing of churches or clergy, or in the ordination of persons to the ministry.

It seems very odd to me that this glaring contradiction in the Constitution is not often addressed in the United Church of Christ, not, at least, in its public discourse, though perhaps it is whispered behind closed ecclesiastical doors or in polity classrooms. In our ecclesiastical practices we act as if both sets of propositions are true, until some local church calls or ordains someone irregularly, whereupon the aggrieved association can cite Paragraph 22 and the irregular congregation can cite Paragraph 18, with the conflicting viewpoints clearly grounded in the Constitution. Something should be changed to achieve a modicum of consistency. If Paragraph 18 is absolutely sacrosanct, then the verb moods in Paragraphs 40, 41, and 22 should be made clearly subjunctive, not left declarative. But since our tendency has been toward strengthening what we call covenant relations between expressions of the church (Article III, Covenantal Relations), it seems clear to me that the changes needed are in Paragraph 18. I propose the following rewording of that paragraph:

> 18. The autonomy of the local community of ministry and mission is inherent in its nature as a community of those who have answered the call of Jesus Christ to follow him in covenant with one another. This principle of autonomy means that the local community manages its

own affairs, which include determining its own organizational structures, adopting its own constitution and bylaws, formulating its own covenants and confessions of faith in consultation with the breadth and diversity of faith traditions in the ecumenical church and the United Church of Christ, calling its pastors and other authorized ministers together with the Association where it holds its standing, determining its own procedures for admitting and dismissing its members, acquiring and managing its property and funds, controlling its own benevolences, and deciding to withdraw from the United Church of Christ without forfeiture of funds and properties, according to the procedures for withdrawal set forth in the Association where it holds its standing.

In this proposed new Paragraph 18 I have tried to soften the tone of suspicion and vigilance in the original wording. I have also tried to clarify those points where the autonomy of the local church is not absolute and never has been, namely, in articulating its own faith, where we do not, in spite of all our diversity, simply accept any belief statement at all, without being able to see it grounded in the heritage of the ecumenical church and the United Church of Christ, and in the procedures we commonly use to call pastors and other authorized ministers set forth in the *Manual on Ministry*.

Strengthening the Role of Conference Minister

The section of Article VIII entitled Associations and Conferences, where the specific responsibilities of conferences appear, should be supplemented with a paragraph on the role of the conference minister. In practice every UCC conference, except for the Calvin Synod where the conference minister is called a bishop, is pastorally led by a conference minister. While their authority is not the formal teaching authority or ruling authority of a bishop in an episcopal polity, they do pastorally care for the churches and ministers in their conferences. This pastoral authority is substantial, even without juridical authority. In addition, the conference minister is a key interpreter of the wider church for the local communities of ministry, and in turn a key interpreter of the cultural settings and local communities of ministry for the national setting of the church. And when discipline is required for a minister or local church, the conference minister often is the one who initiates a review process, even though it is the committee on the ministry that is constitutionally authorized to conduct a disciplinary review.

To take account of this crucial role of pastoral and ecclesial oversight in the United Church of Christ, I propose adding the following new Paragraph 49 in Article VIII:

> 49. A Conference Minister is called to the ministry of oversight by each Conference. The Conference Minister cares for the well-being of local communities of ministry and mission in the Conference and cares for the authorized ministers in that Conference. The Conference Minister takes initiative in situations requiring disciplinary action, as well as communicating the needs and concerns of all expressions of the church to one another.

This new paragraph belongs in the discussion of a re-visioned United Church of Christ ecclesiology because God calls leaders to regional ministries of oversight just as surely as God calls leaders of local communities of ministry and mission. This ministry of oversight is conducted on behalf of communities of those who follow Jesus Christ so that they will be effective in their ministry and mission and so that all expressions of the church may be linked together in covenants of mutual care and admonition.

One More Time — Why Postmodernity Requires a Re-Visioned Ecclesiology

Now that I have outlined re-visioned ecclesiological principles for the United Church of Christ and compared them with current ecclesiological themes, I conclude this chapter by asking again what difference would such a re-visioned ecclesiology make in postmodernity, for the UCC or any mainline denomination. Since in postmodernity there is no settled and secure identity for institutions called churches, as there was in modernity, churches must make their own way by re-visioning the purpose and mission of the church and by entering the cultural fray that characterizes postmodernity with effective uses of mass media communication. That means taking nothing for granted, being clear and confident about shared convictions and callings, and most of all engaging the world with both loving compassion and a prophetic call for justice.

In postmodernity, churches are viewed, if they are viewed at all, as producers and dispensers of spiritual goods and services for people who want them. When churches gain media attention and thus public awareness, it is often over outrageous statements or actions by their leaders, or arrogations of influence and power over social policy claiming divine moral inspiration. Thus churches can be suspected of scheming to regain social control they once held and feared if they resort to the threat of violence or the use of violence, a violence witnessed in the horrors of unchecked church power and visible again today on the world political/religious stage.

In postmodern scholarly circles religious beliefs and practices are viewed as worth serious study and interpretation, according to whatever cultural theory is employed, but certainly not allowing any presumption of universal truth or moral value (not just for religion, but anywhere at all). In modernity, by contrast, religion was assumed to be passing away with the growth of universal knowledge from scientific inquiry. Now religion is back in vogue, but free of any claims of intellectual or moral hegemony. But while diverse religious elements are valued in postmodernity, religious institutions are suspected and feared, which partly explains why postmoderns prefer spirituality over churches.

Ecclesiology is precisely the theological doctrine that bridges this postmodern divide between religions and institutions, by insisting that the very nature of God's presence in human history is a community-creating presence, calling and forming actual communities of love and justice, living with a sense of sacred communion not only with all humankind but also with all creation. If the United Church of Christ can hold fast to its ecclesiological convictions, it can make this counterintuitive claim in the midst of the chaos and polarization of postmodernity, where everything is reduced to visual images and sound bites, where vast oversimplifications replace nuanced analysis, and where a seemingly universal tolerance masquerades private suspicions and hatreds.

But the United Church of Christ will need to change its way of being in the world, and how it understands itself, if its mission of justice and compassion is to go forward in postmodernity. Otherwise we will be viewed as ineffectual liberal ideologues left over from modernity. Re-visioning ecclesiology is one important component of those changes required in postmodernity.

CHAPTER FOUR

A Revised UCC Polity
for Postmodern Times

I N THE LAST CHAPTER I proposed a re-visioned ecclesiology for the United Church of Christ. In this chapter I recommend revisions in UCC polity in light of postmodernity, revisions grounded in that re-visioned ecclesiology. These polity changes will assist the United Church of Christ in becoming more effective in its mission.

While UCC church leaders called for work on ecclesiology soon after the union, these calls were mostly ignored in the wake of urgent justice action required by the social turbulence of the 1960s and 1970s. Ecclesiology is not a compelling concern except for times when the theological meaning of the church is called into question. Polity, on the other hand, has preoccupied the UCC since its beginnings. A paragraph of polity interpretations was added to the Basis of Union in 1948 in order to protect the autonomy of the local church, insisted on by Congregationalists. The *Cadman vs. Kenyon* case (1950–53) concerned the polity question of whether a congregationally organized denomination could legally unite with a church presbyterially organized. Eventually the federal appellate court approved the union. When the UCC Constitution was written and voted on by General Synod, local Congregational–Christian churches, and Evangelical and Reformed synods, in 1961, Paragraph 15 (now 18) guaranteed local church autonomy, while the Paragraphs before and after 15 called for local churches and regional/national expressions of the church to listen to and heed the advice of one another. UCC polity eventually became officially declared a covenantal polity with the adoption in 2000 of Article III, Covenantal Relationships.

This persisting preoccupation with polity has made the word "polity" a shorthand phrase for everything candidates for ministry in the United Church of Christ need to know about their denomination. "Have you had your polity yet?" is a question addressed to anyone preparing for authorized UCC ministry. Polity, in this question, means of course, not just polity, but also UCC history, theology, and ministry. It is telling that the word "polity" carries all this meaning. "Polity" functions as the official shorthand word for the entire UCC tradition, as though theology and history and ministry are somehow captured by polity. It might even appear that in a church welcoming and affirming diversity polity is strangely our one orthodoxy, to which everyone finally must give assent.

If UCC polity is, indeed, our actual orthodox theology of the church, in spite of the ecclesiological clarity found in the Basis of Union, the Constitution, and the Statement of Faith, then my proposals for changing our polity will require, first of all, clarifying what UCC polity actually is, especially its boundaries, so that considering polity changes will not appear to undermine the foundation of the church, which, after all, is not found in our polity but is found in God's gracious invitation to follow Jesus Christ and in our individual and communal decisions to accept that invitation.

To explore UCC polity, I will first describe and characterize our polity as it actually is, omitting as much as possible its larger-than-life mythic proportions, polity defined simply as our form of church organization and governance, not handed down by God but devised by sincerely faithful human responses to Christ's call. Second, I will show how this polity impedes the mission of the church in postmodernity. Finally I will outline polity revisions that will, I believe, strengthen that mission.

The Actual United Church of Christ Polity

We will examine three aspects of the actual polity of the United Church of Christ in order to see it in its entirety: first there is the official polity of covenant relations; then there are the originating polity principles set forth in the Constitution and Bylaws; and third there are the polity practices actually employed. These three polity aspects are substantially in agreement, but they also display incongruities and outright inconsistencies. We will need to understand these incongruities and inconsistencies if we are to imagine revising polity in light of postmodernity.

The Official UCC Polity of Covenant Relations

The official polity of the United Church of Christ is a polity of covenant, or sometimes called a covenantal polity, or a polity of covenant relations. This covenantal characterization of UCC polity was officially set forth in the new constitutional article on covenantal relationships in the revisions of 2000, where Article III, Covenantal Relationships, states: "Each expression of the church listens, hears, and carefully considers the advice, counsel, and requests of others. In this covenant, the various expressions of the United Church of Christ seek to walk together in all God's ways." (This last phrase is from the Salem Covenant of 1629, an early Puritan congregation in Massachusetts Bay.)

This official designation of UCC polity as a polity of covenantal relations intended to fulfill the hopes of founders to create a polity that would be something new on the ecclesial horizon, in which the United Church of Christ would not become, in fact, merely another historical manifestation of either a presbyterian or congregationalist polity. Does this constitutional definition of a covenantal polity fulfill those hopes?

UCC polity documents, particularly in the *Manual on Ministry* and the *Manual on Church* (a document still circulating for study and response), cite the rich meaning of the concept of covenant in the biblical narratives and in the theologies of the German Reformed and English Puritan traditions. But when we speak of covenant in UCC polity discussions nowadays, we intend to emphasize true equality and mutuality among all parts of the church. While God is cited as a covenant partner, a covenant witness, and a covenant-keeper, God's gracious initiation of the covenant, God's blessings on those who keep the covenant, and God's judgment on those who don't — all essential elements in a biblical and Reformed doctrine of covenant — are strangely absent from current UCC discourse, as I noted earlier while discussing ecclesiology.

There are good twenty-first-century theological reasons for hesitating to specify God's blessings and judgments too precisely. Identifying divine judgment with humanly committed atrocities such as ethnic genocides or with natural disasters like floods, fires, earthquakes, or epidemics, is to risk confusing God's will with punitive human condemnations. In the United Church of Christ we typically believe that God aims to increase justice and love, to look for their signs, and to work for those aims. But we are rightly offended when God and alleged covenant-breakers are blamed for disasters not of their own making. It is theologically important, therefore, not to claim too much congruence between biblical and Reformed/Puritan covenant theology and the covenantal polity of the UCC. It is enough to declare that in the radical equality with which we all live in relation to God, and as those who seek to follow Jesus Christ by loving God, creation, and neighbor seeking justice for all, we are embraced by covenantal grace in the church, and that therefore it is our responsibility to maintain covenantal relations.

I hope this more theologically circumspect view of covenant is what we mean when we say that the United Church of Christ has a covenantal polity. I hope that we are speaking about our way of engaging in ministry and mission together, with mutual respect and understanding, among all expressions of the church. And I hope we understand that these are God's ways with us, and we are finally accountable to God, not just one another.

Is this official polity of covenant taking hold in the United Church of Christ? It depends on where you look. Certainly in documents like the *Manual on Ministry* and *Manual on Church*, with the Parish Life and Leadership Team staff in the national setting, among polity teachers and students, with conference and association ministers, and committees on ministry, covenantal polity is well known. But I would guess covenantal polity is little known and even less understood in local churches and other ministry settings until some event brings it to light, something like the resignation of a minister and the search for a new one, or an appeal for denominational support at budget time, or a question raised in a local church about a national UCC stance on a controversial issue attracting media attention. Even then the official polity of covenant may not be cited, only a reminder that all settings of the church speak only for themselves, not for the whole church.

I am aware, however, of instances where "breaking the covenant" is used accusingly, against a person or congregation for doing something that might once have been called wrong or inappropriate. There is a moral code embedded in the concept of a polity of covenant, to be sure, but it is confusing and can be judgmental to accuse someone of breaking the covenant when the actual terms of the covenant are not that clear in the first place.

These observations lead me to conclude that while the official covenantal polity of the United Church of Christ will make its way into our common life and language slowly, it should take hold with theological modesty, refusing to use covenant as a code of moral judgment. If the admonitions of covenantal life — "listens, hears, and carefully considers" (Constitution, Paragraph 6) — are followed, then surely the idea of a covenantal polity will be beneficial to all. But it will take time and practice.

Originating UCC Polity Principles

Alongside the polity of covenantal relations now enshrined in the Constitution, older polity principles appear in the Constitution as well as in the Basis of Union, principles that can be summed up as the absolute autonomy of the local church joined with the obligation to associate with other churches for the well-being of the whole church. The freedom and autonomy of the local church is guaranteed in Paragraph 18. The associative mandates appear in Paragraphs 17 and 19, where every expression (or setting) of the church is called to extend mutual regard for all other settings, and in Paragraphs 40 and 41, where the standing of local churches and ordained ministers is assigned to associations.

In the previous chapter on ecclesiology I pointed out the logical contradiction between Paragraph 18 and the other paragraphs cited. Interpreted literally Paragraph 18 would allow for no interference in the decisions of the autonomous local church if it chose to go its own way. On the other hand, the paragraphs urging associative practices would require that the standing of a local church and its ordained minister(s) be maintained in the association, not just by local churches. How this contradiction is negotiated I will discuss in the next section, on polity practices in the UCC.

First, though, I need to speak of another traditional polity principle in the United Church of Christ, namely, the freedom and autonomy of other expressions of the church along with local churches. Douglas Horton, Executive Minister of the General Council of the Congregational and Christian Churches, argued in lectures given in 1951 that the Council and other such bodies had the legal right to rule themselves and could not be ruled by others. This polity principle was affirmed and then elaborated in Constitutional articles describing associations, conferences, the General Synod, and the covenanted ministries. Though they are not described with the specific attributes of local churches as in Paragraph 18, other settings of the church are still guaranteed the same freedom and autonomy. This principle is explained when we say that the General Synod, or a conference, or an association, or a local church can speak only for itself, not the whole church. This principle seems not widely understood within the UCC or by the general public, however. This confusion may arise from the fact that the General Synod and covenanted ministry boards are composed partly by representatives of conferences and constituency groups, giving the impression that national UCC settings possess no authority of their own, only whatever authority is granted by the groups sending representatives. And that confusion, especially in the general public, may arise from the fact that in other denominations the decisions of such delegated bodies are officially authoritative for the beliefs and practices of their local churches.

I would not want my descriptions of these polity principles of the United Church of Christ to suggest that contradiction and confusion predominate. They are there, but in the ways we practice and interpret our polity principles, their contradictory and confusing qualities are diminished or overlooked altogether. I will explain how that works in the next section.

Polity Practices in the United Church of Christ

The principle of freedom and autonomy prevails in the polity practice of the UCC. Not only local churches but also wider church bodies, from regional to national to international settings, act most of the time as though they possess, by right, the freedom and authority to carry out their mission mandates. This practice works best when there is a foundation of mutual respect and trust, and where there is genuine consultation among settings of the church, especially when an action or statement might be controversial. Only when mission support funds are withheld and/or local churches or individual members leave the denomination do such disagreements test the principles of freedom and autonomy. This prevailing autonomy principle is so deeply embedded in UCC consciousness that we can scarcely imagine any other way of being the church. Several years ago at a meeting I attended a lay UCC member, frustrated with the slow pace of decision making, burst out with, "After all, we're all Congregationalists here!" The ensuing gasps and chuckles reminded him of the historical inaccuracy of his statement. But he really didn't mean, I think, historic Congregationalism. He only meant that we all know, right here and now, that this group has the authority to decide something, so let's just do it. Autonomy prevails!

A second UCC polity practice is that of calling of authorized ministers using the policies and procedures from the Constitution and Bylaws that are detailed in the *Manual on Ministry*. But not all churches and ministries follow that practice. Some conduct their own searches, thinking they can find a better candidate more quickly. The expectation is clear, however, that *Manual* policies and procedures should be followed. When these procedures are not followed, bad things can happen. In a climate of watchfulness about clergy misconduct, where a church does not want to be sued, churches searching for a new minister usually realize that it is safer to use the denominational process, where background checks are mandatory.

A third UCC polity practice consists of the urgent messages from regional and national program agencies to local churches and their ministers. These messages include appeals to support Our Churches Wider Mission and special offerings; urgent requests that local churches study and respond to actions coming before associations, conferences, or the General Synod; urging local churches to use program resources offered by regional or national program agencies; and the call to act on justice issues — donations, messages to government officials, or signing a petition. New communication technologies enable more messages to be sent.

A fourth polity practice, or really, a failure to use a Constitutional tool, but a practice all the same, is the nearly absolute avoidance of the responsibility of associations to "determine, confer, and certify to the standing of local churches in its area," as set forth in Paragraph 40. I say "failure to use" because I do not know of many instances where associations have taken the initiative to review the standing of a local church. Associations, to be sure, respond to requests from newly developing local churches, or from local churches with no previous denominational affiliation or churches leaving another denomination in order to join the United Church of Christ. In these cases associations have devised procedures for reviewing faith statements, constitutions, and bylaws of newly affiliating churches. But I do not know of associations that regularly review and recertify the standing of local churches. Some associations have tried covenant visits to local churches, to engage in a mutual review of the ministry and mission of those churches. But these visits are purely voluntary. If a local church agrees to have such a visit, they may wonder, "Why are you doing this now?" or "What do you want of us?" Other than association-initiated covenant visits or association requests for local church annual reports, I do not know of associations that regularly review the standing of local churches.

Why this hesitation? Surely associations are reluctant to call local churches to account because they fear a reactive defense of local church autonomy against interference by the association, and because they know that wider church linkages are fragile at best. Many questions about a local church's stewardship of its ministry and mission can be imagined — the extent of denominational financial support, awareness and use of denominational programs and resources, seriously paying attention to the recommendations of other settings of the church, sharing their own questions and viewpoints with the wider church, etc. And one can also imagine, as a result of such a periodic review, that an association could consider a range of actions, from full standing renewal, qualified renewal, or even removal from standing. But the bonds of covenant relations would need to be much stronger if associations were to exercise their constitutionally established authority to certify the standing of a local church.

Under the heading of the actual polity of the United Church of Christ, I have discussed the official polity of covenant relations, the originating polity principles of local church autonomy along with mandated and strongly suggested limitations on that autonomy set forth in the Constitution and Bylaws, and the polity practices currently in use. It is easy to see how these polity contradictions and ambiguities allow for both confusion and selective emphasis depending on the interests of those interpreting them. What may be less obvious, however, is how this multidimensional UCC polity impedes its mission moving from modernity into postmodernity. I turn now to these impediments, followed then by proposed polity revisions in light of the new postmodern cultural situation.

UCC Polity Impediments
to Faithful Mission in Postmodernity

Earlier I showed how the ecclesiology and polity of the United Church of Christ became captive to modernity, partly from emerging UCC ecclesial traditions in the Protestant Reformation that paralleled the rise of modernity, and partly from efforts to harmonize faith and modern scientific thought. With the decline of modernity and the emergence of postmodernity, these affiliations put the mission of the UCC at risk because modernity is so embedded in its polity that it is difficult to step back and look more objectively and critically at this polity. Now I will step back and take that critical look, hoping that together we can reconfigure our polity for postmodern times.

The polity of the United Church of Christ should enable the followers of Jesus Christ, gathered into faithful local communities of mission and ministry, where at font and pulpit and table, Christ's followers are renewed and empowered, to witness in word and deed to the justice and loving compassion of God. Where does the actual UCC polity, outlined in the previous section above, impede that mission? Three aspects of UCC modernist polity are particularly inhibiting: First there is the attribution of final authority to the autonomous individual conscience, the autonomous local church, and other equally autonomous regional and national expressions of the church. The second mission impediment of UCC modernist polity is the belief, with all its foundational assumptions, that decisions are best made in a process of communicating information, rational discussion, and persuasion. And the third aspect of UCC modernist polity impeding mission is the conviction that, in the end, the process is more important than the product, if one has to choose. In the next paragraphs I will explain and illustrate these three impediments, and show how postmodernity calls for changes we must seriously consider.

Autonomy and Authority

In modernity authority was wrested from the state and the church and lodged in the individual conscience, enlightened by reason. Individuals could agree to grant authority to local communities entered and sustained voluntarily. Individuals could also grant authority to larger political bodies through their chosen representatives, creating a republican form of democratic polity. But suspicion of authority grew proportionally to the distance separating such offices and assemblies from the local community and the autonomous individuals comprising them. This practice of autonomy and belief in it clearly reflects the practices and beliefs of modernity. Other denominational traditions — Catholic, Orthodox, Anglican, Lutheran, Methodist, Presbyterian — must seem hopelessly archaic or at least premodern in attributing authority to divinely, they believe, appointed offices or assemblies rather than to the authority of autonomous individuals or local churches.

In postmodernity, authority is understood as an amalgam of belief in free personal choices set in the context of multiple reference groups to which one belongs — generational groups, one's social location including racial and cultural heritage, tastes in the arts and fashion, career and lifestyle-based groups, and the celebrities one admires. Supporting this amalgam of diverse authorities is the conviction that the state and its laws should enhance diversity and restrain conformity, but that otherwise the state should not interfere with the way one chooses to live unless those choices harm others. The state also exists to protect this free marketplace of tastes from any wishing to deny it. While it is difficult to summarize a postmodern view of authority, it seems clear that a set of images express the idea of authority better than a political philosophy or an ethical theory. These are images to which one gives loyalty and devotion, and from which arise a sense of life's value. Neither the idea of autonomy or authority would provide any meaningful sense of orientation in postmodernity. Personal choice and reference group influences might seem, from the distance of a modernist observer, to stand for autonomy and authority, but not for postmoderns, who experience life mediated by images, not ideas.

Decisions: Reasons or Feelings?

United Church of Christ polity principles and practices reflect a modernist view that organizational decisions are best made in a process of study, discussion, argument, and counterargument, and then arriving at a decision by consensus or majority vote. Study documents filled with information, policy perspectives, testimonies of expert witnesses along with the views of the laity, and then a time of deliberation are constituents of this decisional process. Assumptions taken for granted in modernity — that people are essentially reasonable, that people possess a native sense of what is best for themselves and their society, and that people will be as objective as they can in considering decisions where there are conflicting views — are not taken for granted in postmodernity.

Postmoderns are much more likely to suspect concealed self-interest in modernist principles and practices, and are at the same time much more likely to be swayed by the emotions, by feelings, by passionate attachments, in deciding how to conduct their lives. The visual images and sound bites of the media world inhabited by postmoderns are far more powerfully motivating than extended discussion and debate, which quickly become dull and boring to postmoderns. These same motivating qualities emanate from celebrities in entertainment and sports, as well as from leaders who may not be creations of the media but who possess those same qualities — energetic, visually attractive, warm, friendly, and able to express things in short and vivid phrases rather than long and complex sentences. These qualities predispose postmoderns to judge quickly rather than engage in lengthy discussions that postpone decisions.

In the United Church of Christ one can see the sharp contrast between modern and postmodern experience by comparing the familiar resolution and pronouncement process at General Synod (or at conference annual meetings) with the Still-Speaking Initiative. The resolution process requires identifying a morally urgent issue, developing a viewpoint on that issue, finding biblical support, citing research findings or expert opinion, and calling for agreement and action. This is a quintessentially modern way of engaging in mission — study, reasoning, persuasion, and a call to action. But in the Still-Speaking Initiative, images and short phrases — the comma, the quotation from Gracie Allen, and the TV commercials — are designed to both teach a lesson and create a feeling about the United Church of Christ. With those images appearing on bumper stickers, shirts, mugs, and pins, and with the same red and black colors, the message and feeling of the commercials are repeated and reinforced. This is a typically postmodern way of engaging in mission, creating a feeling about a God who speaks a word of radical, inclusive hospitality in a world where religions seem to condemn and divide. But the polity of the United Church of Christ favors a modernist, resolution-crafting approach to communicating its mission, with the result that busy people, without the time or background to hear, read, and reflect, tune out the mission message quickly. The polity of the UCC needs to be changed so that the church can claim and encourage an image-rich approach to mission, as it has begun to do with the Still-Speaking Initiative.

Process or Product?

Maximizing participation in decision-making is another polity practice of the United Church of Christ that reflects the firm grip of modernity. This practice is rooted in historic Congregationalism, to be sure, with its belief in the authority of the local church. A justice motivation is also at work in this commitment to being inclusive. Realizing that many people have been excluded from the political process because of race or gender or sexual orientation or ethnicity or age or disability, the moral vision of modernity requires opening the table of decision to greater diversity. If that is not done, then it is business as usual, with power controlled by the privileged few. As a result, modernist polity practice favors large enough groups so that everyone is present and favors a practice that gives greater weight to the process rather than to the product. Informed preparatory work is often discounted or ignored altogether. Previous decisions are reconsidered and often changed. Things bog down and become an endless proceeding where the intended product is lost in the process. Less obvious reflections of this modernist process bias are things like check-ins at meetings where personal reflections are sought and valued, or training in the rules of good group process so that diverse views and feelings will be honored.

Postmoderns value product over process, in contrast with the prevailing UCC preference for good process. From a postmodern perspective, religious organizations exist for programs and mission activities that enable participants to do things of value, for themselves and for the wider world, especially those in need. Postmoderns are reluctant to spend time and energy on committee and board discussions about programs and policies. Institutional structures are not interesting or important except when they get in the way. That is why such widely varied new church forms — megachurches, emergent churches, or cell churches — appeal so strongly to postmoderns. They can enter immediately into program and mission activities, without waiting to establish themselves as persons worthy to be elected to a board or committee in a more traditional (modernist) local church. These postmodern values place an enormous burden on the paid program staff of megachurches to create and operate programs effectively. But with good leadership this system works and even flourishes. Emergent and cell churches are not staff-driven in that way, but their emphasis on participating in program and mission with minimal attention to governance is essentially the same. Governance still happens, of course, but is deliberately kept to a minimum or hidden from view by deference to charismatic leaders.

These postmodern values are worrisome to me and others of my generation, who believe that loyalty to the local church and denomination is an essential aspect of church life, a loyalty deeper, we think, than finding personal fulfillment through finding just the right program or mission. We modernists would acknowledge that institutional loyalty is often tested by poor leaders and bad decisions, but we persist patiently in the belief we are called to carry out our mission through such institutional means. Some postmoderns will have church experiences that will grow into church loyalty of the modernist variety. But the United Church of Christ and other mainline denominations cannot depend on the loyalty of aging modernists like me to maintain local church and denominational institutional structures. Only by revising its present polity principles and practices can the United Church of Christ reach out and engage the coming postmodern generations. Only by amending polity practices and denominational cultures can the UCC shift from favoring the processes of church life to a stronger emphasis on the church's products — its programs and mission.

Proposed Polity Revisions

In the previous section of this chapter I identified three dimensions of United Church of Christ polity: the official polity of covenant, an originating polity of local church autonomy in the context of associational obligations, and polity practices that are now employed in the denomination. In this concluding section of chapter 4, I propose revisions in UCC polity that will, I believe, faithfully reflect a re-visioned ecclesiology and just as faithfully engage the postmodern world more effectively. These revisions will be discussed under the same headings — covenant, autonomy and associational constraints, and practices.

A Revised Official Polity of Covenant

Article III of the United Church of Christ Constitution, Covenantal Relationships (Paragraph 6), defines how the various expressions of the church are to relate to one another. Paragraph 6 calls for consultation, collaboration, mutual honor and respect, and for heeding and considering the advice of all expressions of the church. As noted earlier, the language of this paragraph introduces phrases appearing in Paragraphs 17 and 19 as well as a closing phrase from the New England Salem Church Covenant. This paragraph does not need revising, in my view. But we need to be more careful and modest where we speak about this kind of polity in other places, such as the *Manual on Ministry* and the *Manual on Church*, as well as in writings or speeches employing the covenant theme, so that biblical and theological precedents are not used indiscriminately. While it is entirely proper theologically to cite God as the gracious witness to our humanly devised covenants and as One who holds us accountable for honoring them, we should not cite a polity of covenant as simply equivalent to biblical covenants or Puritan theologies of covenant, which relied on a doctrine of predestination. We should be clear that we have taken an ancient biblical and theological word and used it to express something more contemporary in our sense of how God is in a living and loving relationship with those called to the divine mission by following Jesus Christ. This is not a God who sets up covenants of obedience that weak humans are bound to break and then to be punished for their disobedience by God's wrath. These are covenants of grace, where our human service to God is divinely cherished and prospered, and where our failings and rebellions are laid bare, forgiven, and where we are restored to new life.

I do not want to minimize the importance of taking care about how we speak of a covenantal polity, especially since I am not proposing revisions in Constitutional Paragraph 6. Indeed I hope that with practice and thoughtful reflection we will increasingly speak of a polity of covenant first, before moving on to local church autonomy and its constraints, which is a more familiar and more contested terrain. But we will continue to create covenant practices in which there are real consequences for breaking covenants that go beyond legalism or moralism. While legal remedies for covenant-breaking would be anathema in the United Church of Christ, moral anathemas are not beyond our imagination. But these need to be used with great care, in a covenant of love and mutual support. In the next section on polity principles, I will suggest ways in which such covenant practices can be created without violating our official polity of covenant.

Revised Polity Principles:
Autonomy and Its Constraints

In the previous chapter I proposed a reworded Constitutional Paragraph 18 that would affirm the autonomy of the local church but would also acknowledge the constitutional constraints on autonomy stated in Paragraphs 40 and 41, on the standing of local churches and the standing of ministers. One might expect the continued standing of local churches to be spelled out in some detail in Article V, Local Churches, but in fact its Paragraphs (9 through 19) for the most part address questions of how local churches are comprised and how they become members of the United Church of Christ. Only in Paragraphs 17, 18, and 19 are the relationships of autonomy and its constraints set forth, and, as previously noted, Paragraph 18 guarantees local church autonomy absolutely, while Paragraphs 17 and 19 plead for mutuality between expressions of the church. It is a startling omission that there is no reference to the qualifications required for local churches to continue in standing.

Something of the same imbalance can be seen in the terse wording of Paragraph 41 on the standing of ordained ministers, under Article VIII, Associations and Conferences, when compared with Paragraphs 20 through 30 of Article VI, The Ministry, which explains how ministers gain standing in the United Church of Christ. But nowhere in these paragraphs are the conditions for maintaining standing set forth. Terminating ministerial standing, without further amplification, appears only in Paragraph 41 in Article VIII, Associations and Conferences.

This detailed attention to the ways of gaining standing, by local churches or ministers, with so little attention to the questions of how standing is reviewed and retained might be justified simply by remembering that these are responsibilities of associations, and therefore do not belong in the national UCC Constitution. And indeed it is true that as the *Manual on Ministry* has grown into a large, multichapter document on the practices commonly employed by associations in determining local church standing and the standing of ministers, the *Manual* continues to carry the reminder that these are descriptions of practices in associations, not mandated policies or rules. Over the years many associations have adopted the policies and practices of the *Manual* as their own, resulting in a greater degree of uniform practice in the denomination. Even though these are association responsibilities, I would argue for supplemental language in the key Constitutional paragraphs noted above that would state clearly the responsibility of associations to assess and attest the conditions for continuing in good standing, both for local churches and ministers. Left as they are now, the unbalanced weight of these paragraphs gives the impression that once standing is gained, it is guaranteed for as long as the local church or minister wants it.

Such revisions might read as follows:

40. An Association is that body which determines, confers, certifies to, and regularly reviews the standing of Local Communities of Ministry of the United Church of Christ within its area.

41. An Association is that body which grants, certifies to, transfers, regularly reviews, and terminates the standing of ordained, commissioned, and licensed ministers or ordained ministerial partners in the United Church of Christ within its area.

Though just a few words would be added to each paragraph, revising the Constitution in these ways would foster polity conversations that would deepen a shared sense of mutual responsibility for the well-being of the church, and not just evoke opposition from defenders of local church autonomy.

While the detailed development of such review procedures properly belongs to associations, it is worth remembering, as noted earlier, that some associations already conduct such reviews called covenant visits. Many associations also ask for written annual reports from their minister members to see if further review is warranted.

Regular reviews of local church and ministerial standing in the United Church of Christ need, however, to be further developed. We might create a UCC version of the annual charge conference in the United Methodist Church, where each local church is led through a review of its program and mission, as well as for its pastoral leaders, by the district superintendent. In a UCC version such an annual review could also review the program and mission of a local community of ministry and its pastoral staff, though without the judicial authority present in United Methodist polity. The tone of such a review would be pastoral, but questions about how covenants are kept with the wider church might result in recommendations to committees on ministry, recommendations that could result in an association decision to place a local church on notice or even probation depending on the degree to which a local church pays insufficient attention to its covenant obligations, or pays no attention at all. These covenant obligations might include goals and achievements for mission support; the degree to which the local church does in fact hold in the highest regard decisions or advice emanating from the General Synod, the conference, or the association; the degree of participation in wider settings of the church such as attending meetings of associations and the conference; the degree to which pastoral leaders take part in the wider church; and the degree to which these leaders keep the local church informed about and committed to the wider church.

I also propose an enhanced role for the conference minister in the polity practices of the United Church of Christ. As noted in the previous chapter, neither the Constitution nor the Bylaws speak of such an office. Once again that omission might be explained by the reluctance of the Constitution's framers to determine staffing patterns for conferences and associations. But as I argued in the previous chapter on a re-visioned ecclesiology, the office of conference minister is so crucial for the well-being of a conference, as well as its local communities of ministry and its authorized ministers, that it should not be left out. Indeed the well-being of the entire denomination is substantially entrusted to conference ministers, since they are the ones best able to advocate the concerns and needs of local communities of ministry as well as the concerns and needs of the General Synod, conferences, and associations. Gradually the significance of conference ministers in those complex roles has been increasingly recognized. This office ought to be identified and mandated in the Constitution and Bylaws. First I suggest rewording Paragraph 48, in Article VIII, Associations and Conferences, so that it would read as follows:

> 48. A Conference may retain or secure its own charter, adopt its own constitution, bylaws, and other rules which it deems essential to its own welfare, and call its own Conference Minister, in ways not inconsistent with this Constitution and the Bylaws of the United Church of Christ.

Second, I suggest a rewording of Paragraph 168 of the Bylaws, under Article II, Associations and Conferences, to state the following:

> 168. A Conference calls a Conference Minister to exercise pastoral oversight of its programs and the local communities of ministry within its boundaries. A Conference employs such other salaried personnel as its programs may require.

As I conclude this discussion of the formal polity principles of the United Church of Christ enshrined in its Constitution and Bylaws, I want to raise the question of how these polity principles apply to the organizing and functioning of the national setting of the church — the General Synod along with the General Minister and President, the covenanted ministries with their executive ministers, and all the other related bodies in the national setting. Do the polity principles of local autonomy and its limits apply also to them? At first it might seem they do not apply at all, since local autonomy has to do with local churches and their relations with other church bodies. In spite of that, the same dynamics of local autonomy and its limits seem to be in play in the national setting as well. Though I have not observed these dynamics closely, it seems that national restructuring is driven not alone by the question of how better to serve the churches, but also by questions about how the authority of these national bodies and officers, some of which are defined by mission mandates backed by legally designated endowments, is to be maintained under a doctrine of local autonomy, and how much of its authority is to be a negotiated and shared authority. If I am correct in my judgment that our polity principles and practices favor local autonomy over limits on that autonomy, then I would expect the same bias to be at work in national restructuring efforts. If that is so, then attention needs to be paid, as I am trying to do in this chapter, to claiming and then strengthening limits on autonomy already found in the Constitution.

Proposed Revisions in Polity Practices in the United Church of Christ

I spoke earlier of the polity practice of seeking and calling authorized ministers according to the recommendations of the *Manual on Ministry*. While this practice is not everywhere followed and cannot be mandated, it is widely used because it provides for a standardized process of screening candidates to secure the best possible fit between the candidate and the ministry setting. Local communities of ministry seeking new pastoral leaders employ this Search and Call procedure when they have a vacancy. Their searches are typically staffed by conference ministers or association ministers. In this Search and Call process a local search committee relates not only to an association/conference staff minister, but also with the association committee on the ministry when it comes to determining salary and benefits that are in keeping with conference/association norms. For many local communities of ministry this may be their first introduction to committees on the ministry.

The practices of these committees on ministry require, in my view, a thorough examination and revision if the polity of the United Church of Christ is to facilitate its mission in the twenty-first century. The Constitution and Bylaws do not provide adequate formal foundation for these committees, since they are not even mentioned in Constitutional Article VIII, Associations and Conferences, nor do they appear in the Bylaw Article II, Associations and Conferences. At the same time, Constitutional Article VI, The Ministry, makes it clear that the responsibilities of authorizing and supervising ministers belong to associations, but there is no reference to committees on the ministry.

Then alongside this Constitutional silence appear the Bylaw Paragraphs 102, 106, 141, 145, and 152, in which various responsibilities of association committees on the ministry are described, but with no reference to their foundation or purpose. They are assumed to exist already and can therefore be assigned the responsibilities named in these paragraphs.

This asymmetrical combination of silence about committees on the ministry and the growing number of duties assigned to them can, no doubt, be partly attributed to the process of amending the Constitution when it was determined that the three authorized ministries in the United Church of Christ should be ordained ministers, commissioned ministers, and licensed ministers, and then needing to identify the committees needed to administer discernment and certification. Or, to put it another way, earlier Constitutional and Bylaw references to associations have really come to mean association committees on the ministry.

These committees on the ministry urgently need assistance with their growing workloads, however, more than needing constitutional clarification. It is more than finding enough committee members with enough time to do all this work. It is also a matter of finding committee members with the specialized knowledge required. These committees, in the first place, must create and administer procedures for conducting the discernment process of candidates for authorized ministries, procedures that include candidates' local churches and advisers. Second, these committees must oversee the preparation and education of these same candidates. And third, these committees must conduct regular reviews of the standing of authorized ministers and of the local communities of ministry where they are employed. Included in this review process is the disciplinary review of authorized ministers as spelled out in Section 9 of the *Manual on Ministry.* A typical committee on the ministry is not equipped to do all this. There may be term limits for committee members, meaning that experienced committee members are leaving the committee each year, while new members are taking their places, people who may know little about the work of such committees and may never have heard of or read the *Manual.* My own recent experience is instructive about this workload. Having taught UCC history, theology, and polity for many years, on both seminary campuses and in conference-based programs, I have nevertheless been required to absorb and apply many details of policy and procedure contained in the *Manual* after becoming a member, two years ago, of the committee on the ministry of my own conference, acting as an association. How must it be for someone who has not had all the advantages I have enjoyed?

To address this crisis of excessive workload and insufficient committee competence, I suggest that there should be three ministry committees in each association (or conference acting as an association): a Discernment Committee, a Ministry Formation Committee, and a Review and Discipline Committee. While the proportions of lay and ordained persons might vary, these committees should continue to represent the diversity of UCC constituencies for which we aim in every setting of the church. These three committees, because of their workloads and special competencies required, should not be volunteer committees but should be committees where the members are paid at a professional hourly rate for their services. Each committee would have a defined training/educational program for the committee's work. These training hours would count toward the total number of hours to be reimbursed. Such committee on ministry positions should be paid, semi-professional, part-time positions. Committee chairs should be qualified both to chair and staff these committees professionally. The three committee chairs would periodically consult with the conference minister, but a conference or association minister would not need to staff regular meetings of the committees. While these semi-professional committee members would have term appointments — three or four years, for example — they could serve three successive terms before leaving the committee. Such a procedure would guarantee greater continuity in committee work and reduce the numbers of new persons needing training at any one time. Where might such part-time, paid professionals be found? Recently retired clergy or professors would be one source. Religious or human service professionals putting together several part-time positions or desiring less than full-time work could be another source.

My proposal to pay committee members a stipend can be supported not only because of their heavy workloads (if they do everything they should), but also because of the high quality of the work expected of them. Their tasks of discernment, formation, and review require specialized knowledge that may not be present in a volunteer committee or readily available to it. In each of these three work areas, new occasions are teaching new duties in ways hitherto unimagined, especially as the church moves into postmodernity.

Discernment

Applicants for one of the three authorized ministries in the United Church of Christ — ordained, commissioned, and licensed — come increasingly from diverse and atypical backgrounds where these persons discerned a call to ministry. More applicants nowadays come from mixed denominational or nonchurch backgrounds. The constitutional and *Manual* assumption that an applicant's discernment process begins and is grounded in a local church is often not true at all. Many applicants begin the discernment process by taking courses at a seminary or divinity school (often at the suggestion of a friend or counselor), and then they may decide to work toward the M.Div. degree (required for ordination), or a specialized M.A. (possibly required for commissioning). At some point such persons may discover the United Church of Christ and decide that the UCC is the denomination where they want to be in ministry. Sometimes they come to this realization only when they are near the end of their degree program, or even after they have graduated. What then are they to do? They must find and join a local church, become well enough known there to request that church's endorsement to the committee on the ministry, and then hope that the committee is persuaded of the applicant's worthiness, even though not many in that local church may know the applicant as well as they should in order to recommend them. In addition to that, if it is a local church that has little experience in discerning a call to ministry, the process will be all the more mysterious. Though less likely these days, the judgment of a local church where the applicant is well known may be equally clouded. If it is a favored child of the church, affirmation may be taken for granted and discernment only lightly touched. Or if it has been a difficult child of the church the person's potential for growth may not be recognized. Even though the local church minister may know the *Manual on Ministry*, it would be better if someone with specialized qualifications in discernment could meet with the local church to guide this process.

The qualifications of a discernment specialist would be knowledge of formal ecclesiastical expectations about a valid sense of calling to ministry, knowledge of diverse spiritual autobiographies that explain how the writers became aware of a call to ministry, experience in guiding group conversations with applicants that are both supportive and probing, and a detailed knowledge of the requirements of the committee on discernment, so that both the applicant and local church will know what to do and what comes next. Volunteer members of a committee on the ministry or association/conference ministers may not have the time or expertise required to guide local churches and applicants in this discernment process. A paid professional specialist in discernment who is on the Committee on Discernment can be expected to guide this process so that gifts for ministry are recognized and developmental needs identified for special attention during the discernment process.

Ministry Formation

When a person has been approved for discernment, the committee on the ministry appoints an advisor for the applicant, in keeping with the *Manual on Ministry* and the practices of committees on the ministry. This advisor works with the candidate on preparing an ordination paper, completing the search profile circulated by the Profile Operations Office of the Parish Life and Leadership Team in the national UCC setting, and fulfilling any other committee requirements. Though the candidate may consult this committee-appointed advisor about academic questions, as a rule the candidate depends on the seminary or divinity school where the candidate completed the M.Div. degree for the ministry formational tasks of acquiring the knowledge, skills, and personal characteristics required to be ordained, commissioned, or licensed. For ordination, so long as the applicant has a degree from an accredited theological school and has taken courses in UCC history, theology, and polity, the candidate is presumed to be ready to take the ordination examination conducted by the committee on the ministry.

Two changing circumstances call this familiar pattern into question, and both are related to the transition from modernity to postmodernity. First, seminaries and divinity schools are changing significantly. And second, churches are increasingly recognizing multiple paths to ordained ministry, in which a college and seminary degree may no longer be the only route or even the preferred one. The United Church of Christ has already approved such multiple pathways, based on the Pronouncement on Ministry Issues adopted by General Synod 25 in Atlanta in 2005. Other denominations are exploring similar options. Two circumstances make these explorations increasingly urgent: growing numbers of churches without enough members or money to support full-time professionally educated ministers, and a new mainline denominational commitment to welcome cultural and church traditions that value spiritual qualifications for ordination more than formal educational qualifications. This new awareness about needed spiritual qualifications for ordained church leaders comes, in part, from religious and cultural communities historically marginalized, for example Native Americans or African Americans, and in part from cultures outside the dominant Euro-American heritage, for example, Latin Americans or Asian Americans, church cultures that are growing rapidly in North America.

Seminaries and divinity schools are becoming increasingly multicultural and global in their faculties and courses taught. At the same time, however, and partly because of these gains in diversity, seminaries and divinity schools are less closely tied to educating professional ministers for formerly mainline denominations. Their biblical, historical, theological, and ethics courses are mixtures of traditional resources for ministerial education with, at the same time, religious studies approaches that presume no necessary churchly commitments or personal beliefs on the part of students or professors. Along with these shifts in method and outlook in core academic theological disciplines, courses in the practices of ministry continue to teach both theory and skills and to offer supervised internships in ministry settings. Often, though, these courses seem only distantly related to core theological disciplines. Sometimes these practical courses turn out to be remedial theology or church theology courses.

These new circumstances require traditional committees on the ministry in the United Church of Christ to take on roles previously left to seminaries and divinity schools: designing and administering church-based educational programs in conferences or newly developed regional structures, with local or regional seminaries involved, to be sure. Committees on the ministry must now evaluate seminary and divinity school courses of study to see if they are adequately fulfilling their mission of church leadership formation. And these same committees are called to develop and administer new ministry formation programs grounded in mentoring candidates for ordination, programs that affirm the values of spiritual formation and discernment not widely known or highly regarded in curricula from the dominant culture. It boggles the mind to imagine that volunteer committees on the ministry can add all these new tasks to their current workloads, or to expect that such committees can find the volunteer expertise to create visionary and innovative educational programs. Of the three committees I am recommending in a revised polity, it is this committee on ministry formation that most urgently needs the professional time and expertise to make this plan of multiple paths to ministry attain genuine parity with traditional college and seminary paths. If this parity cannot be achieved, the dominant culture's norm of college and seminary education will still seem the better path, in spite of being less accessible and losing influence. Without such parity conference-based and mentoring-based ministry formation paths will be viewed as second-class.

Review of Standing

As I noted earlier, practices concerning the continued standing of ministers and local churches, while constitutionally authorized, are minimally developed. Associations are usually conscientious and thorough when they admit a new local church as a member of the United Church of Christ. Association committees on the ministry take seriously their responsibility for the transfer of standing when a minister moves into an association from some other association or conference. Some associations request an annual written report from its authorized ministers, reports that a staff person or committee may review to see if continued standing is warranted. And as noted above, some associations conduct covenant visits. A more professionally structured and paid review of standing committee, with the constitutional tools at its disposal, could develop a more disciplined and rigorous process of reviewing the standing of local communities of ministry and ministers holding standing. They could also administer the transfer of standing from one association or conference to another. Currently overloaded committees on the ministry are not able to do any of that effectively.

Conclusion

In this chapter I have recommended changes in the polity of the United Church of Christ to facilitate effective mission in postmodern times. I suggest constitutional and bylaw amendments, greater pastoral authority and initiative for conference ministers, and separating traditional association committees on the ministry into three paid professional committees on discernment, ministry formation, and review.

As I conclude my discussion of these polity revisions, I want to answer two questions that readers may have been asking. How can we afford stipends for part-time professional committee members? And what difference will these polity revisions make in effective mission in a postmodern age?

We can afford a larger budget for professional ministry committee members if we believe such costs are truly required. It will require persuasion and then commitment. Then we will find ways to raise the money. And the process of revising UCC polity will require us to become more fully engaged with postmodernity, to understand it, and to take hold of its unique opportunities for faithful mission.

This transition will take the prayerful work of the whole church. Here is how that work might go: First of all a thoroughly modern denomination like the United Church of Christ needs to explore again its heritage from the ancient church, the medieval church, and the churches of the Protestant Reformation in order to refashion its mission in postmodernity. During modernity these traditions were either radically critiqued or neglected. They were thought to be superstitious or otherworldly. In postmodernity there is a new freedom to explore and embrace traditions of prayer, worship, and the church's mission in the world without such modernist suspicions. The question of whether prayer or worship can really accomplish anything, a typically modernist question, can be set aside in postmodernity and replaced with the question of how prayer and worship faithfully reflect the calling of those who are seeking to follow Jesus Christ. Striving to be intellectually credible to the modern mind can no longer be a compelling objective. And the question of how the followers of Jesus Christ are called to engage the world in postmodernity can no longer be answered by supporting political goals that seem ideologically congruent with church teachings, but where existing disparities of wealth and power go unchallenged, and where diverse cultures are not understood and respected.

I do not mean that the church in postmodernity should huddle in safe enclaves sequestered from the world. But the church needs to engage the world on the church's own terms, so that when the church enters into alliances on behalf of resisting evil and working for justice and peace, the church will be clear about where it can make common cause with others and where it must either dissent or negotiate a more complex relationship of critical support.

To express these cautionary observations more colloquially, a liberal/progressive church in postmodernity, like the United Church of Christ, dare not continue to address the world, as it often did in modernity, in this way: "We know a lot of you folks out there agree with us on [fill in the blank with your favorite issue]. So take a look and come join us!" Such agreements and implied support can no longer to be taken for granted. In fact, even the people with the most developed moral sensitivities may well not join us, but oppose and avoid us when they discover the real costs of discipleship.

I am convinced that the mission of Jesus Christ through the church is far more challenging and revolutionary than we have understood. That is why we urgently need to disentangle ourselves from modernity and vigorously engage postmodernity with the message of God's justice and love and with its mandate to resist the world and work for the transformation of the world. The poor and oppressed await that message and those actions on behalf of justice and peace. Will the United Church of Christ be willing and able to answer that call? That is my hope, and it is the hope that prompted me to write this book.

Afterword

I WAS DRAWN TO THE UNITED CHURCH OF CHRIST even before its founding. While a student at Chicago Theological Seminary in the early 1950s, I rejoiced at the prospect of a denomination like the Congregational and Christian Church, with its commitments to local church autonomy and social justice, and a denomination like the Evangelical and Reformed Church with its commitments to biblical and theological rigor and its devout churchly piety coming together to fulfill a larger ecumenical vision.

But I also had to pay attention to the fears of fellow Congregationalists in the student body and on the faculty that freedom might be imperiled in such a union. After all, the Evangelical and Reformed Church had synods and a General Synod, and surely they would try to exercise authority over local churches, partly because they were accustomed to doing so.

When I joined the faculty of United Theological Seminary of the Twin Cities in 1970, I was drawn into an ongoing conversation with Dean Louis Gunnemann about the emerging ecclesiology and polity of this still new denomination. Coming from the Reformed side of the Evangelical and Reformed denomination, Gunnemann hoped that the UCC would create a new polity for a new church. It was in those conversations that I first heard him speak of a polity of covenant, embracing but going beyond older congregational and presbyterial polities. But I had my doubts. Broken covenants require some kind of consequences. I did not see any real consequences for local churches or ministers who failed to honor their covenant obligations. Gunnemann believed, contrary to my doubts, that over time an ethic of covenantal responsibility could take root and grow in the soil of the new United Church of Christ. To a significant degree his hopes have been realized, particularly if one looks at the increasing volume and detail of the *Manual on Ministry* and its employment by association committees on the ministry. Clergy misconduct and the discipline of authorized ministers (Section 9 in the *Manual*) no doubt have contributed to a growing ethic of covenantal responsibility. But what about local churches and other ministry communities in the United Church of Christ? Has Gunnemann's ethic of covenant responsibility taken root there?

That was the second topic Dean Gunnemann and I discussed frequently. Gunnemann was deeply committed to making the new polity work, and one feature he especially emphasized was the responsibility of the local church to fulfill its role as "the basic unit of the church," set forth in Paragraph 9 of the Constitution. My two previous pastorates before coming to the seminary faculty had not been in local churches, but as a college chaplain and then as a campus minister. I argued that those local communities of ministry were, ecclesiologically, equivalent to the local church; the only substantial difference was that they did not pay their own way. Local churches did pay their own way, and more, supporting the programs and mission of the wider church, including chaplaincies and campus ministries! But I could never convince him on that ecclesiological point.

My conversations with Gunnemann formed a significant part of the backdrop for my Simpson Lecture at Andover Newton Theological School in March of 1996. While my main topic was "Authorizing Ministry in the United Church of Christ," its subtitle was, "Slouching toward Order." I borrowed "slouching" from the poem by William Butler Yeats ("Slouching toward Bethlehem") to indicate that the UCC was moving slowly and reluctantly toward a more ordered church. In that lecture (published in *Prism* 11, no. 2 [Fall 1996]) I raised the possibility (some might have thought it a specter) of committees on the ministry reviewing local churches as well as authorized ministers. I now think that is not only possible but also necessary, as I argue in this book.

I also argue in this book for a change in ecclesiological nomenclature from local church to local community of ministry, as well as arguing for maintaining covenantal relations in ways that will have consequences, not just blaming or shunning. I devoutly hope that the time has come when the United Church of Christ can openly and vigorously discuss such possibilities, and not go on slouching toward order.

So I close with a word of gratitude for all those conversations with Louis Gunnemann, for the opportunities to write and speak about the church across the years, to teach history and polity in seminary and conference settings, and for all I learned from colleagues and friends in the UCC Polity Teachers Network.

Notes

1. Laurene Beth Bowers, *Becoming a Multicultural Church* (Cleveland: Pilgrim Press), 2006.

2. Thomas S. Kuhn, *The Structure of the Scientific Revolution* (Chicago: University of Chicago Press, 1970).

3. Lynn Hunt, *Inventing Human Rights: A History* (New York: W. W. Norton, 2007).

4. Louis H. Gunnemann, *United and Uniting* (New York: United Church Press, 1987).

5. Charles Taylor, *A Secular Age* (Cambridge, Mass.: Harvard University Press, 2007), 80.

6. The Burial Hill Declaration, 1865, can be found in *The Creeds and Platforms of Congregationalism*, ed. Williston Walker (Boston: Pilgrim Press, 1960), 562–64. The Kansas City Platform, 1913, can be found at *www.ucc.org/beliefs/kansas-city-statement-of.html*.

7. David Dunn, *A History of the Evangelical and Reformed Church*, ed. Lowell Zuck (New York: Pilgrim Press, 1990), 85.

8. Louis H. Gunnemann, *The Shaping of the United Church of Christ* (New York: United Church Press, 1977), 25, 29.

9. Carl E. Schneider, "Journey into Union," *A History of the Evangelical and Reformed Church*, ed. Lowell Zuck (New York: Pilgrim Press, 1990), 291.

10. Gunnemann, *The Shaping of the United Church of Christ*, 31–37.

11. Randi Jones Walker, *The Evolution of a UCC Style* (Cleveland: United Church Press, 2005).

12. Ibid., 143.

13. Lewis S. Mudge, *Rethinking the Beloved Community* (Geneva: WCC Publications, 2001), 28.

14. Josiah Royce, *The Problem of Christianity* (Chicago: University of Chicago Press, 1968), 404, 405.

15. David J. Bosch, *Transforming Mission: Paradigm Shifts in Theology of Mission* (Maryknoll, N.Y.: Orbis Books, 1991).

16. "A Mission Framework for the General Synod Committee on Structure," *Report on Restructure to the Twenty-First General Synod of the United Church of Christ*, E4.

17. Ibid.

18. Clyde J. Steckel, "United Church of Christ Ecclesiology at Fifty," *Prism* 21, no. 1 (Spring 2007): 29.